CW00410994

THE ENGLAND FOOTBALL SUPPORTER'S BOOK

This edition published in 2010

Copyright © Carlton Books Limited 2010

Carlton Books Limited
20 Mortimer Street
London W1T 3JW

A CIP catalogue record for this book is available from the British Library

ISBN 978-1- 84732-573-0

This book is an updated abridgement of *The England Football Miscellany*, supplemented by material taken from *The Little Book of England*, *The Biggest Football Pub Quiz Book Ever!* and *The Best Football Songs & Chants Book Ever!* together with new puzzles compiled by David Ballheimer.

Editor: Martin Corteel
Project art editor: Emily Clarke
Production: Kate Pimm

Printed in Great Britain

The publishers would like to thank the following sources for their kind permission to reproduce the pictures in the plate section of this book.

Page 1: PA Archive/Press Association Images
Page 2 (top): Daniel Motz/Press Association Images
Page 2 (bottom): Bob Thomas/Getty Images
Page 3: Billy Stickland/Allsport/Getty Images
Page 4 (top): Paul Popper/Popperfoto/Getty Images
Page 4 (bottom): Ben Radford/Allsport/Getty Images
Page 5: Ben Radford/Allsport/Getty Images
Page 6 (top): Ross Kinnaird/Getty Images
Page 6 (bottom): Sergei Supinsky/AFP/Getty Images
Page 7: Alexander Nemenov/AFP/Getty Images
Page 8 (top): Shaun Botterill/Getty Images
Page 8 (bottom): Clive Brunskill/Getty Images

Every effort has been made to acknowledge correctly and contact the source and/or copyright holder of each picture and Carlton Books Limited apologises for any unintentional errors or omissions that will be corrected in future editions of this book.

THE ENGLAND FOOTBALL SUPPORTER'S BOOK

JOHN WHITE

CARLTON
BOOKS

I would like to dedicate my book to the following England fans and personal friends: Michael "Levi" Bellamy, Granville "Granni" Campbell, William "Bill" Clarkson, Adrian "Addy" Dearnaley, Chris Goodwin, Mike "Big Man" Hartley and last but not least to my editor, Martin Corteel. Finally, I would also like to say a big thank you to my wife, Janice, and our two sons, Marc and Paul, for all of their valued support.

CONTENTS

Chapter 1: England Legends 6

Chapter 2: England in the World Cup 36

Chapter 3: England in the European Championship 64

Chapter 4: England Fantasy Teams 82

Chapter 5: England Lists & Trivia 96

Chapter 6: For Club and Country 130

Chapter 7: England Quotes 152

Chapter 8: England Songs & Chants 164

Chapter 9: England Quizzes & Puzzles 172

Answers 189

CHAPTER

1

ENGLAND LEGENDS

English football has been blessed with some of the world's greatest ever players and managers. How great are these football legends? Six of these 14 were knighted, while two others died before they received this honour, but another knight – the only man to score a World Cup Final hat-trick, no less – doesn't even make the cut here.

From the "Wizard of the Dribble" to "Becks", these men have drawn adoration and adulation, if not always, then for most of their careers. Both Sir Alf Ramsey and Sir Bobby Robson were solid international players, but sealed their legendary status as managers, while Sir Walter Winterbottom was manager for 16 years.

Older readers will need no introduction to any of these players, but Sir Stanley Matthews, Sir Tom Finney, Nat Lofthouse and Billy Wright were household names from the 1940s to the early 1960s, while Bobby Moore and Sir Bobby Charlton were the stars of England's 1966 World Cup glory. From the 1970s to the early 1990s, the feats of Peter Shilton, Gary Lineker and Alan Shearer earned worldwide respect. David Beckham may well be the world's best-known current footballer – in fact he is a global brand – and John Terry is loved for his total commitment to the cause.

David Beckham, OBE

David Robert Joseph Beckham was born on 2 May 1975 in Leytonstone, London. When he was a schoolboy, David attended Tottenham Hotspur's School of Excellence. In 1989, he signed schoolboy forms with Manchester United and became a trainee on 8 July 1991. On 23 September 1992, David made his United debut in a Rumbelows Cup tie at Brighton & Hove Albion.

At the end of the 1995–96 season, a David Beckham-inspired United became the first English Football League Club to win the coveted "Double" twice, following their all-conquering 1993–94 season. On the opening day of the 1996–97 season, David scored perhaps the greatest FA Premier League goal of all time. United visited Wimbledon at Selhurst Park and David sensationally chipped Neil Sullivan in the Wimbledon goal from 55 yards. At club level, David has since gone on to play for Spanish giants Real Madrid and Los Angeles Galaxy in America as well as having two loan spells at Milan in Italy's Serie A.

On 1 September 1996, David made his international debut for England in a 3–1 World Cup qualifier away to Moldova. However, during the 1998 World Cup finals in France, David was sent off against Argentina in a second round match in St Etienne. England lost 4–3 in a penalty shoot-out to end their interest in the competition. Beckham was the target of severe media criticism and public abuse. Undaunted, he bounced back and was instrumental in helping Manchester United to do the "Treble" of Premier League, FA Cup and Champions League the following year.

When Kevin Keegan resigned as England manager in October 2000, caretaker manager, Peter Taylor, made David the team captain for a friendly against Italy. He remained his country's skipper until England were knocked out of the 2006 World Cup.

On 6 October 2001, Beckham almost single-handedly ensured England reached the 2002 World Cup finals. In their final qualifying game, England were trailing Greece 2–1 at Old Trafford with just seconds remaining. Beckham stepped up to fire home an injury time equalizer to book England's place at the finals in Japan/South Korea. At the following summer's finals, Beckham and England gained revenge on Argentina for putting them out of the 1998 World Cup finals. He converted the penalty in Sapporo, Japan, which gave England a 1–0 win over their South American rivals and helped to knock them out in the first round. And, on 12 November 2005, David captained England for the 50th time in a 3–2 friendly win over Argentina in Geneva, Switzerland.

When he played 1–0 in a friendly loss to France in Paris on 26 March 2008 Beckham joined Billy Wright, Sir Bobby Charlton, Bobby Moore and Peter Shilton in winning 100 England caps, and on 28 March 2009, in a 4–0 defeat of Slovakia, he became England's most capped outfield player with 109.

For the Record

Clubs: Manchester United (1993–2003),
  Real Madrid (2003–07), Los Angeles Galaxy (2007–);
  Preston North End (loan, 1995),
  Milan (loan, 2009, 2010)
England appearances: 115
England goals: 17
England debut: vs Moldova (1 September 1996)

Sir Bobby Charlton, CBE, OBE

If you were a child living in the 1960s, apart from Pele, the most famous footballer in the world was Bobby Charlton. Even today the name Bobby Charlton is held in the highest esteem throughout the world, where he is not only remembered for his playing days but as an ambassador for English football.

Bobby Charlton was born on 11 October 1937 in the mining village of Ashington, Northumberland. Bobby's genes dictated that he would be a footballer as his mother, Cissie, was the cousin of Jackie Milburn ("Wor Jackie") the legendary Newcastle United and England centre-forward. In addition, his grandfather and four other uncles were all professional footballers (his uncles George, Jack and Jim played for Leeds United, while his uncle Stan played for Leicester City).

On 9 February 1953 the Manchester United scout, Joe Armstrong, watched Bobby Charlton play, and speaking of the game Joe said: "I had to peer through a mist, but what I saw was enough. This boy is going to be a world beater." About 18 teams wanted to sign him, but Bobby had committed his future to Matt Busby's Manchester United. On 6 October 1956 he made his Manchester United debut against Charlton Athletic at Old Trafford, scoring twice in a 4–2 victory.

Bobby won everything there was to win in the game: an FA Cup winners' medal, three League Championship winners' medals, a European Cup winners' medal and he was voted European Player of the Year in 1966. Bobby made his international debut against Scotland on 19 April 1958 in Glasgow. England won 4–0 and Charlton scored. Less than three months earlier, he had been one of the few United players to survive the Munich air disaster.

In all he played 106 times for England, scoring a record 49 goals, a record that still stands today, and he was a member of the 1966 World Cup winning team. Bobby played in three World Cup finals for England (1962, 1966 and 1970) and was an unused squad member in 1958. The great Sir Matt Busby once said of Bobby: "He has broken all records and won everything possible that there is to win. Yet he has remained completely unspoiled."

Whereas George Best possessed the style and Denis Law was flamboyant, Bobby Charlton was a football machine. He had superb skills, tremendous balance and grace, he was athletic and he possessed a cannon of a shot from up to 35 yards out. From the moment Bobby made his Manchester United debut he was the ultimate professional. In 1973, when Bobby left Old Trafford, he had made a then record 752 appearances and scored 247 goals in an 18-year career of almost unparalleled excellence. He was knighted for his services to football in 1994.

DID YOU KNOW THAT?
Bobby Charlton was the first man to play for England in three decades after World War II, appearing in the 1950s, 60s and 70s.

For the Record

Club: Manchester United (1956–73)

England appearances: 106

England goals: 49

England debut: vs Scotland (19 April 1958)

Sir Tom Finney, OBE

Tom Finney was born on 5 April 1922 in Preston. As a young boy Tom dreamed of becoming a professional footballer, but his father, Alf, insisted that his son should learn a trade and so Tom became an apprentice plumber. In 1940, Tom turned professional, and made his first-team debut later that year. However, Britain was then at war with Germany, and the Football League had been disbanded. During World War II, football in England was played on a regional basis and, in 1940–41, Preston won the Northern Section Championship and also reached the Final of the Wartime Cup, beating Arsenal 2–1 after a replay. It was the only final Tom ever won during his illustrious career but, sadly, wartime football honours are not recognized by the Football Association as a senior football honour. Remarkably, because of the war, Tom became one of only a small number of footballers who made their international debut before they made their full League debut for their club. Towards the end of the war he played for England in a friendly against Switzerland in Berne, but he did not get awarded a cap.

In 1942, Tom was called up with the Royal Armoured Corps, seeing action with the Eighth Army as a tank driver and mechanic, but he still played football on the wartime guest circuit for Bolton Wanderers, Newcastle United and Southampton. On the opening day of the 1946–47, season he made his much-awaited League debut for Preston against Leeds United. On 28 September 1946, Tom made his England debut, scoring in a 7–2 win over Northern Ireland in Belfast. He went on to win 76 caps and score 30 goals. Of the 76 games, England lost only 12, while he won 50 caps before he was on a losing England side – against Scotland.

On 16 May 1948, England humiliated Italy 4–0 in Turin, with Tom scoring twice. Four years later, the Italian side, Palermo, wanted to sign Tom to help them win the Italian Championship. They offered him a £10,000 signing-on fee, a wage of £130 per month, bonuses of up to £100 a game, a Mediterranean villa, a luxury car and free travel to and from Italy for his family. If he had joined them, Preston would also have been given £30,000, but he turned it all down to stay in his beloved Preston.

Tom was an extremely gifted two-footed player, who possessed an explosive shot in both feet. He was quick, had superb balance, was powerful in the air despite his size and could place a pass on a sixpence from almost anywhere on the pitch. He was never booked or sent off. In 1961 he was awarded the OBE and, in 1998, he was knighted for his services to the game.

DID YOU KNOW THAT?

Without doubt, Sir Tom Finney is the most famous player to appear for Preston North End and the club has shown its appeciation to him in many ways. He is the club's lifetime President, their stadium, Deepdale, is on Sir Tom Finney Way and a statue of him stands outside the ground. Inside Deepdale, the main Sir Tom Finney Stand has a photograph of him superimposed on to two blocks of seats.

For the Record

Club: Preston North End (1946–60)

England appearances: 76

England goals: 30

England debut: vs N. Ireland (28 September 1946)

Gary Lineker, OBE

Gary Winston Lineker was born on 30 November 1960 in Leicester. Gary signed for Leicester City in 1976 and in 1978 he made his senior debut for the club. In 1980 he won the Second Division Championship with the Filbert Street side. He won the first of his 80 England caps on 26 May 1984, coming on as a substitute for Tony Woodcock in England's 1–1 draw with Scotland at Hampden Park.

Gary played for the Foxes for seven years before signing for Everton in the summer of 1985 for £800,000. His first and only season with the Toffees saw him rise to national fame, scoring 40 goals in 42 games during the 1985–86 season. However, despite Gary's impressive goals tally Everton were unable to defend the First Division Championship which they'd won the previous season, falling just two points short of city rivals, Liverpool. To add insult to injury, Liverpool won the "Double", beating Everton 3–1 in the FA Cup Final at Wembley, with Gary scoring in the game. Such was the impact that Gary made on Merseyside during the 1985–86 season, he was voted both the PFA Player of the Year and the Football Writers' Player of the Year. At the end of the season Barcelona made Everton an offer they could not refuse and Gary signed for the Catalan club.

Gary won the Golden Boot award at the World Cup in Mexico in 1986, as a Barcelona player. In total Gary played 99 times for Barcelona, scoring 44 times, winning the Spanish Cup in 1988 and the European Cup Winners' Cup in 1989. In the summer of 1989, Gary returned to England and joined Tottenham Hotspur. He stayed at White Hart Lane for three seasons, winning the FA Cup in 1991, under the management of future England coach, Terry Venables. In total, Gary played 105 games for Spurs and scored 67 goals. Gary helped England to the 1990 World Cup semi-finals and when he retired from international football, Gary had scored 48 goals in 80 games for England, one fewer than Bobby Charlton's England record of 49 goals (although Charlton took 26 more caps to score his extra goal). After Spurs, Gary moved to Japan, where he endured an injury-plagued spell in the Japanese J. League with Nagoya Grampus Eight, who were managed by Arsène Wenger.

Despite his long career, Gary was never booked or sent off by a referee. When he retired from playing, Gary almost seamlessly moved into the media, initially as a football pundit before replacing Des Lynam as the BBC's anchorman for *Match of the Day*. Gary has also been a team captain on the sports game show, *They Think It's All Over*. He has long been the feature of TV adverts for Leicester-based Walker's Crisps.

DID YOU KNOW THAT?

Gary Lineker was a fine all-round sportsman who also excelled at cricket and snooker.

For the Record

Clubs: Leicester City (1978–85); Everton (1985–86); Barcelona (1986–89); Tottenham Hotspur (1989–91); Nagoya Grampus Eight (1992–94)

England appearances: 80

England goals: 48

England debut: vs Scotland (26 May 1984)

Nat Lofthouse, OBE

Nathaniel Lofthouse was born in Bolton on 27 August 1925 and played for his hometown Bolton Wanderers for his entire professional career. He signed for Bolton as an apprentice on 4 September 1939, one day after war was declared with Germany. Nat made his debut against Bury on 22 March 1941, in wartime League fixture, scoring twice in a 5–1 win. However, as with many of his contemporaries, he had to wait until he was in his 20s before he could make his debut in the Football League, which didn't resume until the 1946–47 season. Nat made his League debut, against Chelsea on 31 August 1946, again scoring twice but this time Bolton suffered a 4–3 defeat.

Nat made his England debut on 22 November 1950, the first of 33 caps he won for his country, in a game against Yugoslavia at Arsenal Stadium. He scored both England goals in a 2–2 draw. On 25 May 1952, Nat was nicknamed "The Lion of Vienna" by the press after he scored twice in England's 3–2 win over Austria in the Prater Stadium, Vienna. People couldn't believe he put his personal safety to one side, after being knocked out cold by the Austrian goalkeeper as he raced in on goal to score England's winner.

During the 1952–53 season Nat became one of only 12 players to score in every round of the FA Cup, including the Final. However, Bolton lost what became known as "The Matthews Final", to a Stanley Matthews-inspired Blackpool side that beat Bolton 4–3 at Wembley. Nat finally got his hands on the FA Cup when he captained Bolton to victory over a depleted Manchester United side in the 1958 Final and Nat scored both of Bolton's goals in their 2–0 victory.

In 1953, he was named the English Footballer of the Year after topping the First Division goalscoring charts with 30 goals. On 20 May 1956, Nat broke Steve Bloomer's 49-year-old England international goalscoring record by netting his 29th goal after coming on as a substitute for Tommy Taylor in a 5–1 friendly win against Finland in Helsinki (he scored twice in the game).

On 22 October 1958, at the age of 33, Nat made his final appearance for England, against the Soviet Union, and it was only fitting that he scored his 30th goal in England's 5–0 win under the Twin Towers. In January 1960, Nat announced that he was retiring as a result of an ankle injury and, on 17 December 1960, he made his final League appearance for his beloved Bolton Wanderers. He created a club goalscoring record of 285 goals in 503 appearances for Bolton (256 goals in 452 League matches, a remarkable goal average of better than one goal every two games). In 1986, he became Bolton Wanderers' club President.

DID YOU KNOW THAT?

Substitutes were not permitted in competitive football until long after Nat Lofthouse retired. Nevertheless he twice came on as a substitute in internationals and in both games he netted two goals.

For the Record

Club: Bolton Wanderers (1946–60)

England appearances: 33

England goals: 30

England debut: vs Yugoslavia (22 November 1950)

Sir Stanley Matthews, CBE

Stanley Matthews was born on 1 February 1915 in Stoke-on-Trent. In 1929, he joined the Stoke City ground staff aged 14 and was paid £1 per week. Just six weeks after he turned 17, Stan made his first-team debut for Stoke. Matthews made his England debut on 29 March 1934, in a Home International Championship game against Wales in Cardiff. England won 4–0 with Stan scoring. In that same year Stan fell out with his manager and asked for a transfer. The request shocked Stoke's fans so much that local businessmen pleaded with the club to settle the dispute because it was affecting morale and production in their factories. During World War II he served with the RAF.

Another fall-out with Stoke's manager in 1947 resulted in Stan, then aged 32, being sold to Blackpool for £11,500. At Blackpool Stan reached the FA Cup Final three times, losing to Manchester United in 1948 and Newcastle United in 1951. However, perhaps the greatest moment of his career came in the 1953 Final when Blackpool faced Bolton Wanderers at Wembley. More than half a century later, football fans across the world still refer to that match as "The Matthews Final". Blackpool were 3–1 down with 20 minutes remaining. Then the "Wizard of the Dribble" took the game by the scruff of the neck and helped Blackpool to a historic 4–3 win in normal time. It was his cross which was turned into the net by Bill Perry for the winning goal.

On 15 May 1957, Stan wore the England shirt for the 54th and last time in a 4–1 win over Denmark in Copenhagen. In 1961, aged 46, Stan returned to his hometown club, Stoke. He cost the Potters £3,500 but it was money well spent because when he pulled on the red-and-white striped shirt again the club's average attendance rose from 9,000 to a staggering 36,000, such was his appeal. Despite his being 48 years old, Stan still inspired Stoke to promotion back to the First Division in 1963.

Stan always looked after himself, neither drinking nor smoking. He rose before 6.00 a.m. each day to prepare for training and in an era when few players ate carefully, his diet consisted mainly of salads. Stan played his last game for Stoke City aged 50 years and 5 days, and he is the oldest player to have played a match in England's top division, a record that will never be beaten. In 1965, Stan received a knighthood, still the only active footballer so honoured.

Sir Stanley Matthews, CBE, died, aged 85, on 23 February 2000. The people of Stoke turned out to pay homage when his funeral procession passed through the city. His ashes are buried beneath the centre spot at Stoke's Britannia Stadium. Stanley Matthews was the first "Gentleman of Football". In a professional career spanning some 34 years, he played almost 700 league games, and was never cautioned.

DID YOU KNOW THAT?
Stanley Matthews was the first player to be named Football Writers' Association Footballer of the Year (in 1948) and the first to be European Footballer of the Year (aged 41 in 1956).

For the Record
Clubs: Stoke City (1932–47); Blackpool (1947–61); Stoke (1961–65)
England appearances: 54
England goals: 11
England debut: vs Wales (29 March 1934)

Bobby Moore, OBE

Bobby Moore was born Robert Frederick Chelsea Moore on 12 April 1941 in Barking, London. Bobby signed schoolboy forms for the Hammers in August 1956 and, on 2 October 1957, he made his debut for the England Youth Team. In May 1958 he signed as a professional for West Ham United and, four months later, he made his senior debut for the club. Further debuts followed in 1960 (England Under-23s) and in 1961 (FA Cup) before he earned the first of his 108 full international caps for England in a match against Peru on 20 May 1962. England won 4–0 in Lima.

On 20 May 1963, Bobby captained England for the first time when they beat Czechoslovakia 4–2 in Bratislava. He captained England a further 89 times, to equal Billy Wright's record of 90 matches as England captain. With West Ham things went well for the central defender. In May 1964 he captained the Hammers to FA Cup success over Preston North End at Wembley, and the same season was named the Football Writers' Player of the Year.

By now an established player at both club and international levels, Bobby made his European club debut on 23 September 1964 when West Ham met Gantoise of Belgium in the European Cup Winners' Cup. The following May, Bobby captained the Hammers to success in the Final as they beat 1860 Munich 2–0 at Wembley.

On 30 July 1966, Bobby captained England to their greatest ever triumph, the 4–2 extra-time win over West Germany in the World Cup Final at Wembley. It completed a unique hat-trick of cup final victories at Wembley for Bobby. He was voted the 1966 BBC Sports Personality of the Year and the 1966 British Sports Writers' Association

Sportsman of the Year and in 1967, he was awarded the OBE for his services to the game.

On 14 February 1973, Bobby captained England in his 100th international appearance for his country: England won 5–0 in a friendly at Hampden Park. Three days later, Bobby played his 510th game for West Ham, surpassing Jimmy Ruffell's previous record of 509 appearances. On 14 November 1973, he played for, and captained, England for the last time in a 1–0 defeat to Italy at Wembley.

The following March, Bobby joined Fulham and helped them to the 1975 FA Cup Final, where they lost 2–0 to West Ham. He officially retired in 1977 but later played in the North American Soccer League for the Seattle Sounders. Bobby died of cancer on 24 February 1993.

DID YOU KNOW THAT?

On 23 June 1978, Bobby Moore played for Edmonton Black & Gold against Portuguese giants Benfica. The Black & Gold was formed with a view to bringing a North American Soccer League (NASL) franchise to the Canadian city. But they played just five games: against Benfica; twice against AS Roma and two against NASL teams. Bobby's second match, against Poland, was cancelled when the Poles cried off.

For the Record

Clubs: West Ham United (1958–74); Fulham (1974–77); Seattle Sounders (1977)

England appearances: 108

England goals: 2

England debut: vs Peru (20 May 1962)

Sir Alf Ramsey

Alfred Ramsey was born on 22 January 1920 in Dagenham, Essex. In 1946 he made his first-team debut for Southampton, a club he joined just after the end of World War II. Alf won his first England cap in a friendly against Switzerland at Arsenal Stadium on 1 December 1948 which England won 6–0. He went on to win a total of 32 caps for England, 29 in succession, scoring three penalties. In 1949, Tottenham Hotspur paid £29,000 to take him to White Hart Lane, and he became a member of the famous Spurs "push and run" side that won the English Second and First Divisions in successive seasons in 1950 and 1951.

In 1955, Alf hung up his boots and took his first step into management. His first job was as manager of Ipswich Town, a club he took from Division 3 to Division 1 in just six seasons. In their first season in the First Division, in 1961–62, the unfashionable Suffolk club stunned English football by winning the Championship. Ironically, by virtue of Ipswich's Championship success he emulated, as a manager, the feat he achieved as a player, by winning successive Second and First Division Championships.

Alf was not the FA's first choice to succeed Walter Winterbottom as the England manager in 1963. The job was first offered to Jimmy Adamson, Winterbottom's assistant, but Adamson turned the invitation down and Ramsey was appointed. Things did not get off to a good start for Ramsey. In his first game in charge, England travelled to Paris on 27 February 1963, where they lost 5–2 to the French in a European Championship qualifier, Bobby Smith and Bobby Tambling scoring for England.

Alf's greatest moment came in 1966, when he managed England to a dramatic 4–2 World Cup Final win over West Germany at Wembley after extra-time. In 1967 he was given a knighthood. Sir Alf's last game in charge of England was a 0–0 draw against Portugal in Lisbon on 3 April 1974. So, after 113 games as the boss, in which England won more than half of their games, Sir Alf was sacked and Joe Mercer temporarily took charge of England team affairs.

He had one final spell in football management, at Birmingham City in 1977–78, but he couldn't save them from relegation. Sir Alf died on 28 April 1999.

DID YOU KNOW THAT?

Sir Alf Ramsey, uniquely, was involved in England's finest and most infamous international results. He was the right-back when Engand lost 1–0 to the USA in the 1950 World Cup at Belo Horizonte, Brazil and he was manager when England beat West Germany 4–2 to win the World Cup in 1966.

For the Record

Player:

Clubs: Southampton (1946–49); Spurs (1949–55)

England appearances: 32

England goals: 3

England debut: vs Switzerland (1 December 1948)

Manager:

Clubs: Ipswich (1955–63); Birmingham (1977–78)

England matches: 113

First England match: vs France (27 February 1963)

England record (1963–74): P113, W69, D17, L27

Sir Bobby Robson, CBE

Robert William "Bobby" Robson was born in County Durham on 18 February 1933. He began his career at Fulham in 1950, and made 152 appearances, scoring 68 goals, before moving to West Bromwich Albion in March 1956. In five years at West Brom, he played in 239 matches and scored 56 goals. He also became an England international, scoring twice on his debut against France in November 1957. He played three games at the 1958 World Cup finals in Sweden and went on to win 20 caps. In 1962 Bobby returned to Fulham, where he notched up a further 192 games and nine goals.

On turning to management Bobby had brief spells with Vancouver Whitecaps and Fulham before accepting an offer to manage Ipswich Town. Making good use of the club's youth system, he guided Ipswich to First Division runners-up places in both 1981 and 1982. In 1978 they won the FA Cup for the first time and, in 1981, Ipswich won the UEFA Cup.

In 1982 Bobby left Ipswich to succeed Ron Greenwood as England manager. He led England in two World Cup finals (1986 and 1990), and in 1990 took them to the brink of the World Cup Final for the first time since 1966. They lost their semi-final to West Germany after a penalty shoot-out.

Bobby returned to club management at PSV Eindhoven. Having led PSV to consecutive Dutch titles, he took charge of Sporting Lisbon in the summer of 1993, but was sacked in December 1993, despite being top of the league, but after being knocked out of the UEFA Cup. Bobby gained his revenge soon after as his new club FC Porto beat Sporting in the Portuguese Cup Final. He guided Porto to league titles in 1995 and 1996, before moving to Barcelona. Although they won the Spanish Cup and the European Cup Winners' Cup, the championship eluded Barca and Robson was moved upstairs. In September 1999, after a spell back at PSV, Bobby finally returned to England as manager of Newcastle United. However, Sir Bobby was dismissed after Newcastle failed to win any of their opening four games of the 2004–05 season.

Bobby had his first battle with cancer in 1991 and, in 2008, he put his name to the Sir Bobby Robson Cancer Foundation. Five months later, he was informed that his own lung cancer was terminal. Sir Bobby, who was knighted in 2002, died on 31 July 2009 at his home in County Durham. He was 76 years' old. Tributes poured in from the world of football.

DID YOU KNOW THAT?

When Bobby Robson was the manager of Sporting Lisbon he appointed Jose Mourinho as his interpreter. He kept the future Chelsea manager with him when he moved to Porto and Barcelona.

For the Record

Player:

Clubs: Fulham (1950–56, 62–67); WBA (1956–62)

England appearances: 20

England goals: 4

England debut: vs France (27 November 1957)

Manager:

Clubs: Fulham (1968); Ipswich (1969–82); Eindhoven (1990–92, 98–99); Sporting (1992–94); Porto (1994–96); Barca (1996–97); Newcastle (1999–2004)

England matches: 95

First England match: vs Denmark (22 Sept 1982)

England record (1982–90): P95, W47, D18, L30

Alan Shearer, OBE

Alan Shearer was born in Newcastle-upon-Tyne on 13 August 1970. When he was 16 years old at the famous Wallsend Boys Club, Alan was rejected by Newcastle United. Instead the young striker signed for Southampton as an apprentice. In 1988 he made his Southampton debut as a substitute in a game against Chelsea, and a month later he scored a hat-trick in his full debut, against Arsenal. At 17 years and 8 months old, he'd broken Jimmy Greaves's 30-year record as the youngest player to score a hat-trick in top-flight football in England.

On 19 February 1992, Graham Taylor awarded Alan his first full cap and he marked his international debut with a goal against France in England's 2–0 win at Wembley. He was in the England squad for that year's European Championship in Sweden. In 1992, Alan left the Saints and signed for Blackburn Rovers in what, at the time, was a £3.6 million British record transfer fee. It was at Ewood Park that he won his only major club honour, the Premier League title in 1995. At the end of that 1994–95 Championship winning season he was voted the PFA Player of the Year, and was honoured with the same award by his peers two years later.

At the 1996 European Championship, Alan won the competition's Golden Boot with five goals and he helped England qualify for the 1998 World Cup finals. In 1999, Kevin Keegan made him the England captain, such was his importance to the team. Under Keegan, Alan was an ever-present in the England side that qualified for the 2000 European Championship. Despite his heading England's winner against Germany at the finals, England were knocked out of the tournament following defeats to Portugal and Romania.

In the 3–2 loss to Romania in Charleroi, Alan scored his last goal for England in his final appearance for his country. In total, he scored 30 times for England in 63 internationals.

During the summer of 1996, Newcastle paid a world record £15 million to Blackburn to secure his services. On 18 January 2003, Alan scored a goal after only 10 seconds for his hometown club against Manchester City, equalling the fastest ever goal scored in the Premier League, and also equalling the club record for the fastest goal (a Jackie Milburn effort in November 1947). On 4 February 2006, he scored his 201st goal for the Geordies to beat Jackie Milburn's club record of 200.

Alan's final match was a 4–1 victory over local rivals Sunderland on 17 April 2006. It goes without saying that he scored. In his Newcastle career, Alan played in 395 matches and scored 206 goals. One of English football's most prolific marksmen, Alan scored at a rate of better than a goal every other match, finding the net 379 times in 733 appearances.

DID YOU KNOW THAT?

Alan Shearer, with no previous management experience, was appointed boss of Newcastle United on 1 April 2009, in a belated attempt to save the club from relegation. The task proved beyond him and he resigned during that summer.

For the Record

Clubs: Southampton (1988–92); Blackburn Rovers (1992–96); Newcastle United (1996–2006)

England appearances: 63

England goals: 30

England debut: vs France (19 February 1992)

Peter Shilton, MBE, OBE

Peter Leslie Shilton was born in Leicester on 18 September 1949. Peter's place in England's football history is assured as his country's record cap holder. On 25 November 1970, he made the first of his 125 appearances when England beat East Germany 3–1 at Wembley. Twenty years later Peter made his final appearance for England when they lost 2–1 to Italy in Bari, Italy, in a third place World Cup play-off game at the 1990 finals. If it had not been for Ray Clemence (Liverpool and Tottenham Hotspur), Peter could have exceeded 150 caps as Ray won 61 caps between 1975 and 1981.

Peter signed for Leicester City in September 1966 and when he made his first team appearance aged 16, he was so impressive that Leicester sold their England goalkeeper, Gordon Banks, to Stoke City. Peter was the Foxes' youngest ever debutant and he went on to make 286 appearances for his hometown club, actually scoring once. In 1969, aged 19, Peter made his only appearance in the FA Cup Final, when Leicester City lost out to Manchester City.

In November 1974, Peter joined Stoke City, setting a new world record fee for a goalkeeper of £325,000. When he left the Victoria Ground he joined Brian Clough's Nottingham Forest in 1977, where he won the First Division Championship in 1978, and two European Cups in 1979 and 1980. In 1978, Peter was selected as the PFA Player of the Year, and he is the only England international goalkeeper to earn this recognition from his peers. Upon leaving Nottingham Forest, Peter spent five years at Southampton, then a similar period of time at Derby County. He dropped down the divisions to play for Plymouth Argyle for three years before Premier

League Wimbledon signed him as emergency cover. After one game for Bolton Wanderers, Coventry City and West Ham United signed him to short-term contracts before Peter concluded his career at Leyton Orient in 1997.

During the 1982 World Cup finals in Spain, Peter conceded just one goal as England remained unbeaten in their five games. He also represented England at the 1986 World Cup finals in Mexico, suffering the infamous "Hand of God" goal, and played his last England game at the 1990 finals in Italy. In his record 125 international appearances for England, he conceded 83 goals, keeping 65 clean sheets, at 0.66 goals per game.

It was at Leyton Orient that Peter became the first, and to date, only English player to make 1,000 Football League appearances. His 1,000th League game was played at Brisbane Road in December 1996, keeping a clean sheet as Leyton Orient beat Brighton & Hove Albion 2–0. When he retired, Peter had played 1,005 Football League games.

DID YOU KNOW THAT?

Peter Shilton was the last player born in the 1940s to play League football in England.

For the Record

Clubs: Leicester C (1966–74); Stoke C (1974–77); Nottingham Forest (1977–82); Southampton (1982–87); Derby Co (1987–92); Plymouth A (1992–95); Bolton W (1995); Leyton Orient (1996–97)

England appearances: 125

England clean sheets: 65

England debut: vs East Germany (25 November 1970)

John Terry

John George Terry was born on 7 December 1980 in Barking, London and signed for Chelsea's youth team when he was 14 years old. He began his career as a midfielder before Chelsea's reserve team manager asked him to play centre-half, as the team was lacking players in that position. Terry adapted to his new role with ease and made his Chelsea debut on 28 October 1998, as a substitute in a League Cup tie with Aston Villa. He was voted the Chelsea Young Player of the Year in 1998–99, farmed out to Nottingham Forest from March to May 2000 and in 2000–01 he was voted the Chelsea fans' player of the year.

The following season Terry flourished in the heart of the Chelsea defence, and helped the Blues to the 2002 FA Cup Final against Arsenal at the Millennium Stadium, Cardiff. Sadly, a virus put him on the bench for the Final, although he did come on as a second-half substitute.

Another high point of that 2001–02 season for Terry had come on 5 December 2001 when he was given the captain's armband for the first time, in a Premier League game against Charlton Athletic. He also made a number of appearances for the England Under-21 team that season, captaining the team on several occasions. He earned nine caps at this level, scoring once. Terry won his first full England cap as a half-time substitute against Serbia & Montenegro on 3 June 2003, a 2–1 win for England at the Walkers Stadium, Leicester.

When Jose Mourinho was appointed the new Chelsea boss in 2004 his first move was to appoint Terry as club captain. He led the Blues to Carling Cup success in February 2005 and the Premiership title three months later. His peers voted him the PFA Player of the Year in season 2004–05. In 2005–06 he led Chelsea to another title, and to League Cup and FA Cup glory the following season. He played in all five of England's games at the 2006 World Cup finals in Germany and on 10 August 2006, Steve McClaren named Terry as the new England captain. He scored on his debut as the England captain, In a friendly against Greece.

A natural leader, he became one of the most important members of Fabio Capello's England team and was instrumental in helping the squad to reach the 2010 World Cup finals. John's ability to pop up with vital goals was perfectly illustrated on 1 April 2009, when his late strike gave England a crucial 2–1 victory over Ukraine at Wembley. Rio Ferdinand replaced him as England captain on 5 February 2010.

John captained Chelsea to UEFA Champions League runners-up spot in 2008. The following year, he led Chelsea to more FA Cup glory. John received the UEFA Club Football Awards' Best Defender honour in 2005, 2008 and 2009.

DID YOU KNOW THAT?

In May 2007, John Terry became the first captain to lift the FA Cup at the new Wembley Stadium (a 1–0 win over Manchester United), and the following month he became the first player to score a full international goal there, in England's 1–1 draw with Brazil.

For the Record

Club: Chelsea (1998–present)

England appearances: 58

England clean sheets: 6

England debut: vs Serbia & Montenegro (3 June 2003)

Sir Walter Winterbottom, CBE, OBE

Walter Winterbottom was born on 31 March 1913 in Oldham. He trained to be a teacher at Chester Diocesan Training College, qualifying in 1933. During his teaching career, the young Winterbottom played amateur football, and in 1936, he began his professional career with Manchester United as a centre-half.

However, an injury and World War II cut his playing career short. During the 1937–38 season he suffered a spinal injury, and after just 27 games for Manchester United he retired from professional football. However, he did make wartime guest appearances for Chelsea and he played for an FA XI against a Royal Air Force XI at Luton on 6 June 1942. Never capped by England, the closest he came to playing for his country was on 10 October 1942, when he was an unused reserve in England's wartime international against Scotland at Wembley.

In 1946 Walter was appointed national director of coaching with overall responsibility for the England team when official internationals recommenced after the war. His job title was amended to England team manager in May 1947, and Walter remained in that position until Alf Ramsey replaced him in 1962. He became the first person other than the Football Association's Selection Committee to pick the England team.

Walter's first game in charge of England was a 7–2 win over Northern Ireland at Windsor Park, Belfast, in the British Home International Championship on 28 September 1946. England's line-up was: Frank Swift (Manchester City), Laurie Scott (Arsenal), George Hardwick (captain – Middlesbrough), Billy Wright (Wolves), Neil Franklin (Stoke

City), Henry Cockburn (Manchester United), Tom Finney (Preston North End), Raich Carter (Derby County), Tommy Lawton (Chelsea), Wilf Mannion (Middlesbrough) and Bobby Langton (Blackburn Rovers). England's goalscorers were Carter, Finney, Mannion (3), Lawton and Langton.

Walter's worst moment in charge of England came at the 1950 World Cup finals hosted by Brazil. On 29 June, at Belo Horizonte, England were humiliated by the United States of America, the goal being scored by Larry Gaetjens. On 2 November 1962, Walter took charge of England for the last time in a Home International Championship game against Wales at Wembley Stadium. England won 4–0 with goals from John Connelly, Alan Peacock (2) and Jimmy Greaves. In total, Walter Winterbottom took charge of England for 138 games and had a 56 per cent win average.

In 1963, he was awarded an OBE, a CBE followed in 1972 and in 1978 he was given a knighthood. Sir Walter Winterbottom died on 16 February 2002, aged 88. In 2005 he became the fourth former England manager to be elected to the Football Hall of Fame.

DID YOU KNOW THAT?

Walter Winterbottom is the only England manager who was neither a full England international as a player nor ever a manager of a club in domestic football.

For the Record

England matches: 138

First England match: vs Northern Ireland
(28 September 1946)

England record (1946–62): P138, W77, D28, L33

Billy Wright, CBE

William Ambrose Wright was born on 6 February 1924 in Ironbridge, Shropshire, England. As a boy he supported Arsenal, but when he heard that Wolverhampton Wanderers were advertising in the local newspaper for young boys to attend trials, he made his way aged 14 to Molineux to try his luck. He signed on as a member of the ground staff team in July 1938. Still only 14, he made his debut for Wolves in a B Team game against Walsall Wood in the Walsall Minor League.

When he first arrived at the club, the Wolves' manager, Major Frank Buckley, wasn't convinced of Billy's football ability and told him that he did not think that he would make it as a professional footballer. In 1939, shortly after the outbreak of war, Billy made his Wolves debut in a 2–1 victory at Notts County and shortly after the end of World War II, Billy was made the captain of Wolves.

Billy led Wolves to FA Cup glory in 1948–49, and the First Division Championship in 1953–54, 1957–58 and 1958–59. On 28 September 1946, Billy won his first international cap for England in a 7–2 win over Northern Ireland at Windsor Park, Belfast, the first official post-war international.

Billy graced the Three Lions shirt for a further 13 years (missing only three games) and during that time, he won 105 caps and scored three times. England won 60 of the games, drew 23 and lost 21 with one game abandoned. Billy played his last game for England in their 8–1 win over the USA in Los Angeles on 28 May 1959. His record of captaining England 90 times was later equalled by Bobby Moore, while his record 105 caps stood for 20 years until it was broken by Bobby Charlton in 1970.

Billy Wright, captain of Wolves and England, was a one-club man throughout his career, and one of football's greatest ambassadors. In the 541 games he played for Wolves and the 105 times he pulled on an England shirt, he was never cautioned. In 1952 he was voted the Footballer of the Year and played his last League game for Wolves in the penultimate match of their 1958–59 Championship winning season, a 3–0 win over Leicester City at Molineux. He was awarded the CBE in 1959 and retired before the start of the 1959–60 season. Billy said farewell to his adoring fans in their annual pre-season "Colours v Whites" game at Molineux.

Billy was Arsenal manager from 1962 to 1966 before moving into television, first as a pundit then an executive. A year after retiring from television, he accepted an invitation from new Wolves chairman Jack Hayward to join the board. On 3 September 1994, Billy passed away after a fight against cancer. Today a statue of Billy stands as proud as the man himself outside his beloved Molineux.

DID YOU KNOW THAT?

One month after the end of the 1958 World Cup finals, England captain Billy Wright married Joy Beverley, the eldest of the internationally famous trio of singing sisters.

For the Record

Club: Wolverhampton Wanderers (1939–59)

England appearances: 105

England goals: 3

England debut: vs Northern Ireland (28 Sept. 1946)

CHAPTER
2

ENGLAND IN
THE WORLD CUP

Forty-four years ago, England were on top of the world, and they have spent most of the time since then trying to regain the World Cup they won in 1966.

England were not eligible to play in the first three tournaments, having withdrawn their membership of FIFA, and their first attempt on the World Cup, in 1950, was nothing short of disastrous, including a 1–0 defeat against the USA in Belo Horizonte, Brazil.

Since then, England have played in 12 of the 15 finals, and advanced from the first group stage on all but one of those occasions – and that was a play-off loss. But, 1966 apart, England have not been able to dine at football's top table. The closest they came to a second Final was the penalty shoot-out heart-break against West Germany at Italia 90.

Three times World Cup penalty shoot-outs have been a prelude to England misery, something that only Romania and Italy can match, but the Italians did win a World Cup Final on penalties. In fact, defeat and controversy seem to follow England almost every time our World Cup dreams are dashed – remember Gordon Banks's illness in 1970, "the Hand of God" in 1986, the disallowed golden goal in 1998 and the injury blight in 2006?

World Cup Finals – Brazil 1950

England's first World Cup participation came in 1950 when the finals were held in Brazil. It was the first tournament after the end of World War II and only 13 countries participated in the finals. Notable absentees included Germany and Hungary (who would contest the 1954 Final), Argentina and those in Eastern Europe.

England qualified by winning the Home International Championship in the 1949–50 season, and they should have been joined in Brazil by runners-up Scotland. But the Scots refused to take their place because they were not prepared to travel to Brazil if they weren't British champions and as they lost 1–0 to England at Hampden Park in April 1950, Rob Bentley scoring, they finished runners-up.

Joining England in Group 2 of the first round were Chile, Spain and the United States of America. England won their opening game 2–0 on 25 June against Chile. Four days later one of the biggest World Cup shocks in history took place at the Estádio Independencia, Belo Horizonte, when the USA sensationally beat England 1–0 with a goal from Larry Gaetjens. England lost their final group game 1–0 to the group winners, Spain, in the magnificent Estádio Maracanã, Rio de Janeiro. England finished runners-up in the group, which was not good enough to see them progress to the next stage.

The tournament was, for the only time, decided not by a Final, but by a final group. Uruguay broke the home fans' hearts by beating Brazil 2–1 in the final, and coincidentally decisive match at the Maracanã, in front of 199,954 fans. It was also the first time that the trophy itself was named "the Jules Rimet Cup" in honour of the famous FIFA official.

FIRST ROUND, GROUP 2

25 JUNE 1950, RIO DE JANEIRO, 30,000

England (1) **2**   v   **Chile** (0) **0**

(Mortensen 27,

Mannion 51)

England: Williams, Ramsey, Aston, Wright, Hughes, Dickinson,

Finney, Bentley, Mannion, Mortensen, Mullen.

29 JUNE 1950, BELO HORIZONTE, 10,000

USA (1) **1**   v   **England** (0) **0**

(Gaetjens 38)

England: Williams, Ramsey, Aston, Wright, Hughes, Dickinson,

Finney, Bentley, Mannion, Mortensen, Mullen.

2 JULY 1950, RIO DE JANEIRO, 74,000

Spain (0) **1**   v   **England** (0) **0**

(Zarra 48)

England: Williams, Ramsey, Eckersley, Hughes, Wright, Dickinson,

Matthews, Baily, Milburn, Mannion, Mortensen.

GROUP 2 – FINAL TABLE

	P	W	D	L	F	A	Pts
Spain	3	3	0	0	6	1	6
England	**3**	**1**	**0**	**2**	**2**	**2**	**2**
Chile	3	1	0	2	5	6	2
USA	3	1	0	2	4	8	2

Winners only qualified for final group stage.

DID YOU KNOW THAT?

Some England newspapers thought that the result which came over the wire from Belo Horizonte was incorrect, so they printed the final score as England 10, USA 0.

World Cup Finals – Switzerland 1954

At the 1954 World Cup finals in Switzerland, England were drawn in Group D with Belgium, Italy and the host nation. It was the first time television covered the finals. There was an unusual system in the first round group stage because although each group had four teams, each nation would play only two matches; the two highest and lowest countries in the FIFA rankings would not play each other. It meant England would not have to face 1934 and 1938 winners Italy and Switzerland and Austria did not play each other.

In their opening game, on 17 June, England drew 4–4 with Belgium after extra-time in the St Jakob Stadion, Basel. Ivor Broadis and Nat Lofthouse both scored twice for England, who led 3–1 with 20 minutes remaining. England's second game was three days later, against the hosts, Switzerland, at the Wankdorf Stadion, Berne, a game England won 2–0 with goals from Ivor Broadis and Denis Wishaw. It was enough for England to finish on top of their group with three points. In their quarter-final game England were drawn to face the holders, Uruguay. Sadly for Walter Winterbottom's team England lost 4–2 in the St Jakob Stadion. Carlos Borges gave Uruguay a fifth-minute lead and although Lofthouse soon equalised, goals from Obdulio Varelia and Juan Schiaffino either side of half-time put *La Celeste* in charge. Tom Finney pulled a goal back after 67 minutes, but Javier Ambrois sealed the victory with 12 minutes remaining.

The Final was played on 4 July at the Wankdorf Stadion in front of 62,472 fans and it saw tournament favourites Hungary take on West Germany. Although the Magyars took a 2–0 lead, the Germans fought back to win 3–2 and end Hungary's four-year unbeaten run.

17 JUNE 1954, BASEL, 40,000

England (2) **4**　　v　　**Belgium** (1) **4**

(Broadis 26, 63,　　　(Anoul 5, 71, Coppens 67,

Lofthouse 36, 91)　　　Dickinson o.g. 94)

England: Merrick, Staniforth, Byrne, Wright, Owen,

Dickinson, Matthews, Broadis, Lofthouse, Taylor, Finney.

20 JUNE 1954, BERNE, 50,000

England (1) **2**　　v　　**Switzerland** (0) **0**

(Mullen 43, Wishaw 69)

England: Merrick, Staniforth, Byrne, Wright, McGarry,

Dickinson, Finney, Broadis, Wishaw, Taylor, Mullen.

GROUP C – FINAL TABLE

	P	W	D	L	F	A	Pts
England	**2**	**1**	**1**	**0**	**6**	**4**	**3**
Switzerland*	2	1	0	1	2	3	2
Italy	2	1	0	1	5	3	2
Austria	2	0	1	1	5	8	1

*Switzerland defeated Italy 4–1 in a play-off.

QUARTER-FINAL

26 JUNE 1954, BASEL, 35,000

Uruguay (2) **4**　　v　　**England** (2) **2**

(Borges 5, Varela 39,　　　(Lofthouse 16, Finney 67)

Schiaffino 46, Ambrois 78)

England: Merrick, Staniforth, Byrne, Wright, McGarry, Dickenson,

Matthews, Broadis, Lofthouse, Wilshaw, Finney.

DID YOU KNOW THAT?

The 1954 finals were held in Switzerland to celebrate FIFA's 50th anniversary. Their headquarters are in Geneva.

World Cup Finals – Sweden 1958

The 1958 World Cup finals were hosted by Sweden. For the first time, all four British sides qualified and they were put in different groups in the first round. England were paired with the Soviet Union, Brazil and Austria.

England's opening match was against the USSR at the Nya Ullevi Stadion in Gothenburg and it ended in a 2–2 draw, goals from Derek Kevan and a Tom Finney penalty coming after England had trailed 2–0 ten minutes into the second half. Three days later, also at Ullevi, England drew 0–0 with the 1950 World Cup runners-up, Brazil. In their final group game at the Ryavallen Stadion in Boras, England drew 2–2 with Austria. Karl Koller and Andreas Körner twice gave Austria the lead, but Johnny Haynes and Kevan netted levellers. The three draws gave England a share of second place in the group, resulting in a play-off against the USSR for a quarter-final place. Anatoly Ilin scored the only goal after 69 minutes in Gothenburg to send the USSR through and England out.

The tournament not only saw Brazil go on to win the World Cup for the first time, but also the world was introduced to the precocious talent of Edson Arantes do Nascimento, better known as Pele. The 17-year-old scored his first World Cup goal, the only one of the match, in the quarter-final against Wales, grabbed a 23-minute hat-trick in the 5–2 semi-final defeat of France and added another two in the Final as Brazil beat the hosts 5–2 in a pulsating contest.

Another player who took the headlines in Sweden was French striker Just Fontaine, who set an all-time single-tournament record by scoring 13 goals.

FIRST ROUND, GROUP 4

8 JUNE 1958, GOTHENBURG, 45,000

Soviet Union (1) **2**   v   **England** (0) **2**

(Simonian 13, Ivanov 55)   (Kevan 66,

                                    Finney (pen) 85)

England: McDonald, Howe, Banks, Clamp, Wright,
Slater, Douglas, Robson, Kevan, Haynes, Finney.

11 JUNE 1958, GOTHENBURG, 30,000

Brazil (0) **0**   v   **England** (0) **0**

England: McDonald, Howe, Banks, Clamp, Wright,
Slater, Douglas, Robson, Kevan, Haynes, A'Court.

15 JUNE 1958, BORAS, 16,800

England (0) **2**   v   **Austria** (2) **2**

(Haynes 56, Kevan 73)   (Koller 16, Körner 70)

England: McDonald, Howe, Banks, Clamp, Wright,
Slater, Douglas, Robson, Kevan, Haynes, A'Court.

GROUP C – FINAL TABLE

	P	W	D	L	F	A	Pts
Brazil	3	2	1	0	5	0	5
Soviet Union	3	1	1	1	4	4	3
England	**3**	**0**	**3**	**0**	**4**	**4**	**3**
Austria	3	0	1	2	2	7	1

PLAY-OFF

17 JUNE 1958, GOTHENBURG, 23,180

Soviet Union (0) **1**   v   **England** (0) **0**

(Ilin 69)

England: McDonald, Howe, Banks, Clayton, Wright,
Slater, Brabrook, Broadbent, Kevan, Haynes, A'Court.

World Cup Finals – Chile 1962

The World Cup finals were staged in South America for the third time in 1962 and the host nation was Chile. England, still managed by Walter Winterbottom, were the sole British representative and they were drawn in a first phase group with Argentina, Bulgaria and Hungary.

In their opening game at the finals, at the Estadio Braden in Rancagua on 31 May, England lost 2–1 to the 1954 runners-up Hungary. Ron Flowers scored from the penalty spot after an hour to cancel out Lajos Tichy's 17th-minute opener, but Florian Albert scored what proved to be the winner a minute after Flowers's equaliser. Next up for England were Argentina, also in Rancagua, and another penalty from Flowers, plus goals from Bobby Charlton and Jimmy Greaves gave England a three-goal lead on their way to a 3–1 victory. A goalless draw with Bulgaria in the Estadio Braden on 7 June was enough for England to progress to the quarter-finals. On 10 June 1962, they travelled to the Estadio Sausalito, Viña del Mar, to face the defending champions Brazil. Although Pele was out injured England still lost 3–1, with Gerry Hitchens getting England's goal. Garrincha scored twice for Brazil and Vava got the other as England's dreams of glory died.

Brazil were almost unstoppable and they saw off hosts Chile 4–2 in the semi-final to set up a Final against Czechoslovakia. The two teams had drawn 0–0 in an earlier meeting in the first round group stage, but this time Brazil made no mistake, winning 3–1, despite trailing to an early goal from Josef Masopust. Amarildo equalised before Zito and Vava scored in the final 21 minutes to give Brazil their second World Cup success.

FIRST ROUND, GROUP 4

31 MAY 1962, RANCAGUA, 7,938

Hungary (1) **2**   v   **England** (0) **1**

(Tichy 17, Albert 61)   (Flowers pen 60)

England: Springett, Armfield, Wilson, Moore, Flowers, Norman, Douglas, Greaves, Hitchens, Haynes, Charlton.

2 JUNE 1962, RANCAGUA, 9,794

England (2) **3**   v   **Argentina** (0) **1**

(Flowers pen 17,   (Sanfilippo 81)

Charlton, Greaves 67)

England: Springett, Armfield, Wilson, Moore, Flowers, Norman, Douglas, Greaves, Peacock, Haynes, Charlton.

7 JUNE 1962, RANCAGUA, 5,700

England (0) **0**   v   **Bulgaria** (0) **0**

England: Springett, Armfield, Wilson, Moore, Flowers, Norman, Douglas, Greaves, Peacock, Haynes, Charlton.

GROUP 4 – FINAL TABLE

	P	W	D	L	F	A	Pts
Hungary	3	2	1	0	8	2	5
England	**3**	**1**	**1**	**1**	**4**	**3**	**3**
Argentina	3	1	1	1	2	3	3
Bulgaria	3	0	1	2	1	7	1

QUARTER-FINAL

10 JUNE 1962, VIÑA DEL MAR, 17,736

Brazil (1) **3**   v   **England** (1) **1**

(Garrincha 31, 59, Vava 53)   (Hitchens 38)

England: Springett, Armfield, Wilson, Moore, Flowers, Norman, Douglas, Greaves, Hitchens, Haynes, Charlton.

World Cup Finals – England 1966

England hosted the 1966 World Cup finals and became the first post-war hosts to claim the Jules Rimet Trophy. They were drawn in a group with Uruguay, France and Mexico, all matches being at Wembley. A dull 0–0 draw with Uruguay. was followed by 2–0 defeats of Mexico, Bobby Charlton and Roger Hunt scoring, and France, Hunt netting both goals.

Argentina were England's quarter-final opponents and the only goal of a spiteful game came from Geoff Hurst, but most memorable was the dismissal of Argentina's captain Antonio Rattin and his reaction to it. England faced Portugal at Wembley in the semi-finals on 26 July, winning a hard fought match 2–1 with Bobby Charlton netting both goals.

On 30 July 1966, Geoff Hurst earned undying fame by scoring a World Cup Final hat-trick. England beat West Germany 4–2 afer extra time. Helmut Haller gave Germany the lead. Hurst equalised and Martin Peters put England 2–1 up. In the last minute Wolfgang Weber forced extra-time and Hurst added two more goals to win the Cup for England.

FIRST ROUND, GROUP 1

11 JULY 1966, WEMBLEY, 75,000

England (0) **0**   v   **Uruguay** (0) **0**

England: Banks, Cohen, Wilson, Charlton J., Moore,
Stiles, Ball, Charlton R., Connelly, Greaves, Hunt.

16 JULY 1966, WEMBLEY, 85,000

England (1) **2**   v   **Mexico** (0) **0**

(Charlton R. 37, Hunt 75)

England: Banks, Cohen, Wilson, Charlton J., Moore,
Stiles, Peters, Charlton R., Paine, Greaves, Hunt.

20 JULY 1966, WEMBLEY, 92,500

England (1) **2**   v   **France** (0) **0**

(Hunt, 37, 75)

England: Banks, Cohen, Wilson, Charlton J., Moore,
Stiles, Peters, Charlton R., Paine, Greaves, Hunt.

GROUP 1 – FINAL TABLE

	P	W	D	L	F	A	Pts
England	**3**	**2**	**1**	**0**	**4**	**0**	**5**
Uruguay	3	1	2	0	2	1	4
Mexico	3	0	2	1	1	3	2
France	3	0	1	2	2	5	1

QUARTER-FINAL

23 JULY 1966, WEMBLEY 88,000

England (0) **1**   v   **Argentina** (0) **0**

(Hurst 78)

England: Banks, Cohen, Wilson, Charlton J., Moore,
Stiles, Peters, Charlton R., Ball, Hurst, Hunt.

SEMI-FINAL

26 JULY 1966, WEMBLEY 90,000

England (1) **2**   v   **Portugal** (0) **1**

(Charlton R. 30, 80)   (Eusebio pen 82)

England: Banks, Cohen, Wilson, Charlton J., Moore,
Stiles, Peters, Charlton R., Ball, Hurst, Hunt.

FINAL

30 JULY 1966, WEMBLEY 93,000

England (1) **4**   v   **West Germany** (2) **2**

(Hurst 18, 101, 120,   (Haller 12, Weber 89)
Peters 78)

England: Banks, Cohen, Wilson, Charlton J., Moore,
Stiles, Peters, Charlton R., Ball, Hurst, Hunt.

World Cup Finals – Mexico 1970

Mexico hosted the first of its two World Cup finals in 1970. On 2 June 1970 England beat Romania 1–0 in their opening game and then faced the mighty Brazil and lost 1–0 in a game that will forever be remembered for Gordon Banks's unbelievable save from a forceful downward header from the legendary Pele. Jairzinho scored Brazil's winner and went on to become the first player in World Cup history to score in every game of a finals tournament. England then beat Czechoslovakia 1–0 in their final group game and qualified for the quarter-finals.

On 14 June England played West Germany, in the quarter-final at Estadio Guanajuato, León. Alan Mullery put England ahead in the 31st minute and Martin Peters added a second goal in the 49th minute to give them a 2–0 lead. Franz Beckenbauer then pulled a goal back for West Germany in the 68th minute and two minutes later Sir Alf Ramsey substituted a tiring Bobby Charlton in the hope of keeping him fresh for the semi-final. However, Alf's plan backfired on him as Beckenbauer, with Charlton absent, started to exert his own influence on the game. Uwe Seeler equalized for the West Germans in the 76th minute to send the game into extra-time and bring back memories of their extra-time Final encounter at Wembley four years earlier. In the 108th minute Gerd Müller scored West Germany's winner past Peter Bonetti, who was deputizing for an ill Gordon Banks in the England goal. West Germany gained their revenge.

Brazil's form got better and better. They crushed Peru in the quarter-finals, did likewise against Uruguay in the last four, and were unstoppable against Italy. Pele, Gerson, Jairzinho and Carlos Alberto all scored in the 4–1 Final win.

FIRST ROUND, GROUP 3

2 JUNE 1970, GUADALAJARA, 50,560

England (0) **1**   v   **Romania** (0) **0**

(Hurst 65)

England: Banks, Newton (Wright, 51), Cooper, Labone, Moore,
Mullery, Ball, Charlton R., Peters, Lee (Osgood, 75), Hurst.

7 JUNE 1970, GUADALAJARA, 66,843

Brazil (0) **1**   v   **England** (0) **0**

(Jairzinho 59)

England: Banks, Wright, Cooper, Labone, Moore, Mullery,
Ball, Charlton R. (Bell, 63), Peters, Lee (Astle, 63), Hurst.

11 JUNE 1970, GUADALAJARA, 49,292

England (0) **1**   v   **Czechoslovakia** (0) **0**

(Clarke pen 50)

England: Banks, Newton, Cooper, Charlton J., Moore, Mullery, Bell,
Charlton R. (Ball, 65), Peters, Clarke, Astle (Osgood, 65).

GROUP 3 – FINAL TABLE

	P	W	D	L	F	A	Pts
Brazil	3	3	0	0	8	3	6
England	**3**	**2**	**0**	**1**	**2**	**1**	**4**
Romania	3	1	0	2	4	5	2
Czechoslovakia	3	0	0	3	2	7	0

QUARTER-FINAL

14 JUNE 1970, LEON, 23,357

West Germany (0) **3**   v   **England** (1) **2**

(Beckenbauer 68,   (Mullery 31, Peters 49)

Seeler 76, Müller 108)

England lost after extra-time

England: Bonetti, Newton, Cooper, Labone, Moore, Mullery,
Ball, Charlton R. (Bell, 70), Peters (Hunter, 81), Hurst, Lee.

World Cup Finals – Spain 1982

At the 1982 World Cup finals, hosted by Spain, England were drawn in Group D in the first round with Czechoslovakia, France and Kuwait. England's first game was on 16 June, a 3–1 win over France. England followed this up with a 2–0 win over Czechoslovakia and a 1–0 win over Kuwait. All of England's Group D games were played in Estadio San Mamés, Bilbao, and they progressed to the second final group stages after topping Group D with maximum points.

England now found themselves in the same group as the host nation, Spain, and old rivals West Germany. Despite not losing a single game at the 1982 finals, England still failed to qualify for the quarter-finals after two goalless draws saw them finish group runners-up to West Germany.

West Germany made it all the way to the Final, where they lost 3–1 to Italy. Rossi, Tardelli and Altobelli scored for the Italians, with Brietner getting a late consolation goal for the Germans.

FIRST ROUND, GROUP D

BILBAO, 16 JUNE 1982, 44,172

England (1) **3** v **France** (1) **1**

(Robson 1, 67, Mariner 83) (Soler 24)

England: Shilton, Mills, Sansom (Neal, 90), Thompson,
Butcher, Coppell, Robson, Wilkins, Rix, Mariner, Francis.

BILBAO, 20 JUNE 1982, 41,123

England (0) **2** v **Czechoslovakia** (0) **0**

(Francis 62,

(Barmos o.g. 66)

England: Shilton, Mills, Butcher, Thompson, Butcher, Coppell,
Robson (Hoddle, 46), Wilkins, Rix, Mariner, Francis.

BILBAO, 25 JUNE 1982, 39,700

England (1) **1**   v   **Kuwait** (0) **0**

(Francis 27)

England: Shilton, Neal, Mills, Thompson, Foster,
Coppell, Wilkins, Hoddle, Rix, Mariner, Francis.

GROUP D – FINAL TABLE

	P	W	D	L	F	A	Pts
England	**3**	**3**	**0**	**0**	**6**	**1**	**6**
France	3	1	1	1	6	5	3
Czechoslovakia	3	0	2	1	2	4	2
Kuwait	3	0	1	2	2	6	1

SECOND ROUND, GROUP 2

29 JUNE 1982, MADRID, 75,000

West Germany (0) **0**   v   **England** (0) **0**

England: Shilton, Mills, Sansom, Thompson, Butcher,
Coppell, Robson, Wilkins, Rix, Mariner, Francis (Woodcock, 77).

5 JULY 1982, MADRID, 75,000

Spain (0) **0**   v   **England** (0) **0**

England: Shilton, Mills, Sansom, Thompson, Butcher, Robson,
Wilkins, Rix (Brooking, 65), Woodcock (Keegan, 64), Mariner, Francis.

GROUP 2 – FINAL TABLE

	P	W	D	L	F	A	Pts
West Germany	2	1	1	0	2	1	3
England	**2**	**0**	**2**	**0**	**0**	**0**	**2**
Spain	2	0	1	1	1	2	1

DID YOU KNOW THAT?

Both Kevin Keegan and Trevor Brooking made their only
World Cup finals appearances as substitutes against Spain.

World Cup Finals – Mexico 1986

In 1986, Mexico staged the World Cup for the second time, thereby becoming the first country to host two World Cup finals. England opened their campaign with a 1–0 defeat by Portugal followed by a disappointing 0–0 draw with Morocco. Then England beat Poland 3–0 thanks to a Gary Lineker hat trick. All of England's opening group games were played in Estadio Tecnológico, Monterrey. England finished second in the group and qualified for the second round.

England's opponents in the second round were Paraguay in Estadio Azteca, Mexico City. Two goals from Gary Lineker and one from Peter Beardsley gave England a 3–0 win and passage to the quarter-finals. Argentina stood between England and a place in the semi-finals but the infamous "Hand of God" goal from Diego Maradona put an end to England's dream. England lost 2–1 in Estadio Azteca with Gary Lineker scoring his sixth goal of the tournament, the most goals scored by an England player at a World Cup finals. It earned him the tournament's Golden Boot award.

Argentina, inspired by Maradona, defeated Belgium in the semi-final and went on to win the World Cup, beating West Germany 3–2 in the Final, with goals from Jose-Luis Brown, Jorge Valdano and Jorge Burruchaga.

FIRST ROUND, GROUP F

MONTERREY, 3 JUNE 1986, 23,000

Portugal (0) **1**   v   **England** (0) **0**

(Carlos Manuel 76)

England: Shilton, Stevens G., Sansom, Butcher, Fenwick, Hoddle, Robson (Hodge, 79), Wilkins, Waddle (Beardsley, 79), Hateley, Lineker.

MONTERREY, 6 JUNE 1986, 33,500

England (0) **0**   **v**   **Morocco** (0) **0**

England: Shilton, Stevens G., Sansom, Butcher, Fenwick, Hoddle,
Robson (Hodge, 4), Wilkins, Waddle, Hateley (Stevens G.A., 76), Lineker.

MONTERREY, 11 JUNE 1986, 23,000

England (3) **3**   **v**   **Poland** (0) **0**

(Lineker 9, 14, 34)

England: Shilton, Stevens G., Sansom, Butcher, Fenwick, Hoddle, Reid,
Steven, Hodge, Beardsley (Waddle, 75), Lineker (Beardsley, 85).

GROUP F – FINAL TABLE

	P	W	D	L	F	A	Pts
Morocco	3	1	2	0	3	1	4
England	3	1	1	1	3	1	3
Poland	3	1	0	2	1	3	2
Portugal	3	1	0	2	2	4	2

SECOND ROUND

MEXICO CITY, 18 JUNE 1986, 98,728

England (1) **3**   **v**   **Paraguay** (0) **0**

(Lineker 31, 73,
Beardsley 56)

England: Shilton, Stevens G., Sansom, Martin, Butcher, Hoddle,
Reid (Stevens G.A., 58), Steven, Hodge, Beardsley (Hateley, 80), Lineker.

QUARTER-FINAL

MEXICO CITY, 22 JUNE 1986, 114,580

Argentina (0) **2**   **v**   **England** (0) **1**

(Maradona 51, 54)   (Lineker 80)

England: Shilton, Stevens G., Sansom, Butcher, Fenwick, Hoddle,
Reid (Waddle, 64), Hodge, Steven (Barnes, 74), Beardsley, Lineker.

World Cup Finals – Italy 1990

In the first phase of Italia '90, England were drawn in Group F with Egypt, Holland and the Republic of Ireland. England drew 1–1 with the Republic of Ireland, drew 0–0 with Holland and beat Egypt 1–0 to end up top of their group.

England needed extra-time to beat both Belgium, 1–0, and Cameroon 3–2, to reach the semi-finals. Facing West Germany in Turin, after 90 minutes the score was 1–1, Gary Lineker scoring England's equaliser. It went to a penalty shoot-out, with England losing 4–3. Stuart Pearce and Chris Waddle failed with their kicks. England lost the third-place play-off game to Italy, 2–1 in Bari. In the Final, Andy Brehme scored with a penalty as West Germany beat Argentina 1–0.

FIRST ROUND, GROUP F

CAGLIARI, 11 JUNE 1990, 35,238

England (1) **1**   v   **Republic of Ireland** (0) **1**

(Lineker 8)   (Sheedy 73)

England: Shilton, Stevens (G.), Pearce, Walker, Butcher, Waddle, Robson, Gascoigne, Barnes, Beardsley (McMahon, 69), Lineker (Bull, 83).

CAGLIARI, 16 JUNE 1990, 35,267

England (0) **0**   v   **Holland** (0) **0**

England: Shilton, Parker, Pearce, Walker, Butcher, Wright, Robson (Platt, 64), Waddle (Bull, 58), Gascoigne, Barnes, Lineker.

CAGLIARI, 21 JUNE 1990, 34,959

England (0) **1**   v   **Egypt** (0) **0**

(Wright 64)

England: Shilton, Parker, Pearce, Walker, Wright, Waddle (Platt, 86), McMahon, Gascoigne, Barnes, Lineker, Bull (Beardsley, 84).

	P	W	D	L	F	A	Pts
England	**3**	**1**	**2**	**0**	**2**	**1**	**5**
Holland	3	0	3	0	2	2	3
Republic of Ireland	3	0	3	0	2	2	3
Egypt	3	0	2	1	1	2	2

SECOND ROUND

BOLOGNA, 26 JUNE 1990, 34,520

England (0) **1**   **v**   **Belgium** (0) **0**

(Platt 119)

England win after extra-time

England: Shilton, Parker, Pearce, Walker, Butcher, Wright,

Waddle, McMahon (Platt, 71), Gascoigne,

Barnes (Bull, 74), Lineker.

QUARTER-FINAL

NAPLES, 1 JULY 1990, 55,205

England (1) **3**   **v**   **Cameroon** (0) **2**

(Platt 25, Lineker 2 pens 83, 105)   (Kunde pen 61, Ekeke 65)

England win after extra-time

England: Shilton, Parker, Pearce, Walker, Butcher (Steven, 73),

Wright, Waddle, Platt, Gascoigne,

Barnes (Beardsley, 46), Lineker.

SEMI-FINAL

TURIN, 4 JULY 1990, 62,628

England (0) **1**   **v**   **Germany** (0) **1**

(Lineker 80)   (Brehme 60)

Germany won 4–3 on penalties after extra-time

England: Shilton, Parker, Pearce, Walker, Butcher (Steven, 70),

Wright, Waddle, Platt, Gascoigne,

Beardsley, Lineker.

World Cup Finals – France 1998

France hosted the 1998 World Cup finals between 10 June and 12 July. England were in the same group as Tunisia, Romania and Colombia and they got off to a good start with a 2–0 win over Tunisia in the Stade Velodrome in Marseille on 15 June, Alan Shearer and Paul Scholes scoring late in each half. A week later, in the Stade Municipale, Toulouse, England lost 2–1 to Romania, despite Michael Owen scoring his first World Cup finals goal to cancel Fiorel Moldovan's earlier effort. Dan Petrescu was Romania's match-winner in the last minute. Goals from Darren Anderton and David Beckham in the first half-hour were enough to give England a 2–0 win over Colombia in Stade Felix Bollaert, Lens, and see them through to the last 16. Scotland's World Cup adventure ended with a 3–0 first round defeat to Morocco.

In their second phase match England were drawn to face Argentina at Stade Geoffroy-Guichard, Saint-Etienne, on 30 June. The game was a tense affair and ended 2–2 at the end of 90 minutes. England were reduced to 10 men early in the second half when Beckham was red-carded for flicking his foot at Diego Simeone. Extra-time was played but no further goals were added. The game had to be decided by a penalty shoot-out which England lost 4–3, David Batty failing from the spot.

The hosts had not been particularly impressive early in the tournament and their fans had been subdued, but the whole of France seemed to come alive after a 1–0 defeat of Paraguay in the second round. Zinedine Zidane showed he was the world's best player with some great displays, especially in the Final against Brazil. He scored twice, and Emmanuel Petit got the other goal as France won 3–0.

FIRST ROUND, GROUP G

MARSEILLE, 15 JUNE 1998, 54,587

England (1) **2** **v** **Tunisia** (0) **0**

(Shearer 43, Scholes 89)

England: Seaman, Campbell, Le Saux, Southgate, Adams, Batty, Ince, Scholes, Anderton, Sheringham (Owen, 85), Shearer.

TOULOUSE, 22 JUNE 1998, 33,500

Romania (0) **2** **v** **England** (0) **1**

(Moldovan 47, Petrescu 90)   (Owen 79)

England: Seaman, Campbell, Le Saux, Southgate, Adams, Batty, Ince (Beckham, 32), Scholes, Anderton, Sheringham (Owen, 72), Shearer.

LENS, 26 JUNE 1998, 38,100

Colombia (0) **0** **v** **England** (2) **2**

(Anderton 20, Beckham 29)

England: Seaman, Neville G., Le Saux, Adams, Campbell, Beckham, Ince (Batty, 83), Scholes (McManaman, 73), Anderton (Lee, 79), Owen, Shearer.

GROUP G – FINAL TABLE

	P	W	D	L	F	A	Pts
Romania	3	2	1	0	4	2	7
England	**3**	**2**	**0**	**1**	**5**	**2**	**6**
Colombia	3	1	0	2	1	3	4
Tunisia	3	0	1	2	1	4	1

SECOND ROUND

ST ETIENNE, 30 JUNE 1998, 30,600

Argentina (2) **2** **v** **England** (2) **2**

(Batistuta pen 6, Zanetti 45)   (Shearer pen 10, Owen 16)

England lost 4–3 on penalties after extra time

England: Seaman, Neville G., Le Saux (Southgate, 71), Campbell, Adams, Beckham, Ince, Merson (Scholes, 78), Anderton (Batty, 97), Owen, Shearer.

World Cup Finals – Korea/Japan 2002

The 2002 World Cup finals were co-hosted by Japan and South Korea. England were placed in first phase Group F along with Argentina, Nigeria and Sweden and would play all their matches in Japan. In their opening game on 2 June, England drew 1–1 with Sweden in the Saitama Stadium, Saitama, Sol Campbell scoring for England. Five days later England faced bitter rivals, Argentina, in the Sapporo Dome, Sapporo, Japan. David Beckham gained revenge for England and himself when he scored the only goal of the game from the penalty spot after Michael Owen had been fouled. In their final group game England drew 0–0 with Nigeria in the Nagai Stadium, Osaka, a result which was enough to put England into the next stage as runners-up behind Sweden.

On 15 June, goals from Rio Ferdinand, Owen and Emile Heskey gave England all they needed to beat Denmark 3–0 in the second round in the Niigata Stadium, Niigata. However, in the quarter-finals, despite leading through Owen, England lost 2–1 to Brazil in the Shizuoka Stadium, Shizuoka.

Brazil went on to win their fifth World Cup, defeating Germany 2–0 in an uninspiring Final, with both the goals scored by Ronaldo, the tournament's leading marksman.

FIRST ROUND, GROUP F

SAITAMA, 2 JUNE 2002, 52,271

England (1) **1**   v   **Sweden** (0) **1**

(Campbell 24)   (Alexandersson 59)

England: Seaman, Mills, Cole A., Campbell, Ferdinand,
Beckham (Dyer, 63), Hargreaves, Scholes,
Vassell (Cole J., 73), Owen, Heskey.

SAPPORO, 7 JUNE 2002, 35,927

Argentina (0) **0**   **v**   **England** (1) **1**

(Beckham (pen) 44)

England: Seaman, Mills, Cole A. (Bridge, 85), Ferdinand, Campbell, Beckham, Scholes, Butt, Hargreaves (Sinclair, 19), Owen (Vassell, 77), Heskey (Sheringham, 69).

OSAKA, 12 JUNE 2002, 44,864

Nigeria (0) **0**   **v**   **England** (0) **0**

England: Seaman, Mills, Cole A. (Bridge, 85), Ferdinand, Campbell, Beckham, Scholes, Butt, Sinclair, Owen (Vassell, 77), Heskey (Sheringham, 69).

GROUP F – FINAL TABLE

	P	W	D	L	F	A	Pts
Sweden	3	1	2	0	3	3	5
England	**3**	**1**	**2**	**0**	**2**	**1**	**5**
Argentina	3	1	1	1	2	2	4
Nigeria	3	0	1	2	1	3	1

SECOND ROUND

NIIGATA, 16 JUNE 2002, 40,582

Denmark (0) **0**   **v**   **England** (3) **3**

(Ferdinand 5, Owen 22, Heskey 44)

England: Seaman, Mills, Cole A., Ferdinand, Campbell, Sinclair, Beckham, Scholes (Dyer, 49), Butt, Owen (Fowler, 46), Heskey (Sheringham, 69).

QUARTER-FINAL

SHIZUOKA, 21 JUNE 2002, 47,436

England (1) **1**   **v**   **Brazil** (1) **2**

(Owen 23)   (Rivaldo 45, Ronaldinho 50)

England: Seaman, Mills, Cole A. (Sheringham, 80), Ferdinand, Campbell, Beckham, Scholes, Butt, Sinclair (Dyer, 56), Owen (Vassell, 79), Heskey.

World Cup Finals – Germany 2006

Germany hosted the 18th FIFA World Cup in 2006. England opened in Group B against Paraguay in the Waldstadion Frankfurt on 10 June and an own goal from Carlos Gamarra gave England a 1–0 win. Two late goals, from Peter Crouch and Steven Gerrard, brought a 2–0 victory over Trinidad & Tobago in Nuremburg. England and Sweden had already guaranteed their qualification before they met in Cologne. The match was marred by Michael Owen's serious knee injury after just 90 seconds, but goals from Joe Cole and Gerrard brought a 2–2 draw.

On 25 June, David Beckham's free-kick gave England a 1–0 win over Ecuador in Stuttgart to set up a quarter-final against Portugal in Gelsenkirchen. There were no goals in 120 minutes, with England's low point being Wayne Rooney's red card for stamping on Ricardo Carvalho. Yet again England lost out on penalties, Portugal going through 3–1.

The final was between Italy and France. Zinedine Zidane's penalty was cancelled out by Marco Materazzi, but the match will be remembered for Zidane's red card for head-butting Materazzi in the chest. The match went to penalties where France's David Trezeguet hit the bar, while the Italians converted all five kicks to win 5–3. The decisive fifth penalty came from left-back Fabio Grosso.

FIRST ROUND, GROUP B

FRANKFURT, 10 JUNE 2006, 48,000

England (1) **1**   v   **Paraguay** (0) **0**

(Gamarra o.g. 3)

England: Robinson, Neville, Ferdinand, Terry, Cole A., Beckham, Lampard, Gerrard, Cole J. (Hargreaves, 82), Owen (Downing, 56), Crouch.

England (0) **2**　　**v**　　**Trinidad & Tobago** (0) **0**

(Crouch 83, Gerrard 90)

England: Robinson, Carragher (Lennon, 58), Terry, Ferdinand, Cole A., Beckham, Lampard, Gerrard, Cole J. (Downing, 75), Owen (Rooney, 58), Crouch.

COLOGNE, 20 JUNE 2006, 45,000

England (1) **2**　　**v**　　**Sweden** (0) **2**

(Cole J. 34, Gerrard 85)　　　　(Allback 51, Larsson 90)

England: Robinson, Carragher (Lennon, 58), Ferdinand (Campbell, 56), Terry, Cole A., Beckham, Lampard, Hargreaves, Cole J., Rooney (Gerrard, 69), Owen (Crouch, 4).

GROUP B – FINAL TABLE

	P	W	D	L	F	A	Pts
England	3	2	1	0	5	2	7
Sweden	3	1	2	0	3	2	5
Paraguay	3	1	0	2	2	2	3
Trinidad & Tobago	3	0	1	2	0	4	1

SECOND ROUND

STUTTGART, 25 JUNE 2006, 52,000

England (0) **1**　　**v**　　**Ecuador** (0) **0**

(Beckham 60)

England: Robinson, Hargreaves, Terry, Ferdinand, Cole A., Beckham (Lennon, 87), Carrick, Gerrard (Downing, 90), Lampard, Cole J. (Carragher, 77), Rooney.

QUARTER-FINAL

GELSENKIRCHEN, 1 JULY 2006, 52,000

England (0) **0**　　**v**　　**Portugal** (0) **0**

England lost 3–1 on penalties after extra-time

England: Robinson, Neville, Ferdinand, Terry, Cole A., Hargreaves, Beckham (Lennon, 52, [Carragher, 119]), Lampard, Gerrard, Cole J. (Crouch, 65), Rooney.

WC Qualifiers – South Africa 2010

England were in UEFA Group 6 for the 2010 FIFA World Cup qualifying competition. Ukraine and Croatia – who had ended England's Euro 2008 hopes – appeared to be England's main rivals and the rest of the group comprised Andorra, Belarus and Kazakhstan. Under coach Fabio Capello, England made no mistake in qualifying. The expected victory in Andorra was followed by a 4–1 crushing of Croatia in Zagreb, with Theo Walcott grabbing a hat-trick. Kazakhstan, twice, Belarus, Ukraine and Andorra, again were all beaten to send England into summer 2009 with their place in South Africa almost certain. The 5–1 demolition of Croatia at Wembley ensured it, making the 1–0 defeat in Ukraine no more than a blip. A 3–0 defeat of Belarus at Wembley completed the programme. England's 34 goals in ten games was the best average of all 32 qualifying teams. Wayne Rooney top-scored with nine goals.

BARCELONA, 6 SEPTEMBER 2008
Andorra (0) **0**   **v**   **England** (0) **2**
(J. Cole 48, 55)

ZAGREB, 10 SEPTEMBER 2008
Croatia (0) **1**   **v**   **England** (1) **4**
(Mandzukic 78)   (Walcott 26, 59, 82, Rooney 63)

WEMBLEY, 11 OCTOBER 2008
England (0) **5**   **v**   **Kazakhstan** (0) **1**
(Ferdinand 52, Kuchma o.g. 64,   (Kukeyev 68)
Rooney 76, 86, Defoe 90)

MINSK, 15 OCTOBER 2008
Belarus (1) **1**   **v**   **England** (1) **3**
(Sitko 28)   (Gerrard 11, Rooney 50, 75)

WEMBLEY, 1 APRIL 2009

England (1) **2**   **v**   **Ukraine** (0) **1**

(Crouch 29, Terry 85)   (Shevchenko 74)

ALMATY, 6 JUNE 2009

Kazakhstan (0) **0**   **v**   **England** (2) **4**

(Barry 40, Heskey 45
Rooney 72, Lampard pen 77)

WEMBLEY, 10 JUNE 2009

England (3) **6**   **v**   **Andorra** (0) **0**

(Rooney 4, 39, Lampard 29,
Defoe 73, 75, Crouch 80)

WEMBLEY, 9 SEPTEMBER 2009

England (2) **5**   **v**   (0) **1 Croatia**

(Lampard pen 7, 59,   (Eduardo 71)
Gerrard 18, 67, Rooney 77)

DNEPROPETROVSK, 10 OCTOBER 2009

Ukraine (1) **1**   **v**   (0) **0 England**

(Nazarenko 30)

WEMBLEY, 14 OCTOBER 2009

England (1) **3**   **v**   (0) **0 Belarus**

(Crouch 4, 76, Wright-Phillips 60)

GROUP 6 – FINAL TABLE

	P	W	D	L	F	A	Pts
England	**10**	**9**	**0**	**1**	**34**	**6**	**27**
Ukraine	10	6	3	1	21	6	21
Croatia	10	6	2	2	19	13	20
Belarus	10	4	1	5	19	14	13
Kazakhstan	10	2	0	8	11	29	6
Andorra	10	0	0	10	3	39	0

CHAPTER 3

ENGLAND IN THE EUROPEAN CHAMPIONSHIP

It would be fair to say that England have been the continent's biggest under-achievers when it comes to Europe's premier international tournament. England have never actually won a knock-out match in a European Championship finals tournament since it expanded in 1980 (Spain were beaten in Euro 96 in a penalty shoot-out after the match had ended goalless). Indeed, qualification has often proved far from straightforward, with embarrassing failures in 1984 and 2008.

And, when we actually get to the finals tournament, three matches and a plane home has been the norm. Since 1968, when a controversial semi-final defeat against Yugoslavia ended dreams of a World Cup/European Championship double, England did not reach the knock-out stages until they were hosts in 1996 and we all know what happened then.

The World Cup has seen England suffer a succession of unfortunate exits, but the same cannot be said of the Euro championships. Since 1980, England have won just six of 18 matches; twice they have gone out of tournaments after failing to win a single match. Despite this, the second-highest goalscorer in the European Championship history is English. Alan Shearer's seven goals are two behind Michel Platini.

European Championship 1968

England did not participate in the first European Championship, hosted by France in 1960, and in 1964 England failed to advance from the preliminary stages of the competition for the finals in Spain. England's first taste of European Championship finals matches came in Italy in 1968. UEFA allowed the Home International Championship for the 1966–67 and 1967–68 seasons to serve as the preliminary competition for qualification to the 1968 Championship.

England topped the group, ahead of Scotland, Wales and Northern Ireland. To qualify for the finals in Italy, England had to beat Spain in a final qualifying game. On 3 April 1968 England won 1–0 at Wembley thanks to a Bobby Charlton goal, and in the return match, at Madrid's Estadio Santiago Bernabeu on 8 May, goals from Charlton again, Roger Hunt and Martin Peters gave England a 3–1 victory.

At the finals, England lost 1–0 to Yugoslavia in Florence. The match was made famous because Alan Mullery became the first England player to be sent off when he retaliated to a foul. The only goal came in the last five minutes, from Yugoslavia's captain, Dragan Dzajic. The third-place play-off was played in Rome on 8 June, as a curtain-raiser before the Final, and England gained a measure of consolation by defeating the Soviet Union, 2–0, with goals from Bobby Charlton and Geoff Hurst.

Italy met Yugoslavia in the Final and the game ended 0–0. In the replay two days later, the host nation beat the Yugoslavs 2–0 in the Stadio Olimpico, Rome, with goals from Luigi Riva and Pietro Anastasi.

SEMI-FINAL

5 JUNE 1968, FLORENCE, 21,800

Yugoslavia (0) **1**   v   **England** (0) **0**

(Dzajic 86)

England: Banks, Newton, Wilson, Labone, Moore,

Ball, Hunter, Mullery, Peters, Hunt, Charlton.

THIRD-PLACE PLAY-OFF

8 JUNE 1968, ROME, 50,000

England (1) **2**   v   **Soviet Union** (0) **0**

(Charlton 40, Hurst 63)

England: Banks, Wright, Wilson, Stiles, Labone,

Moore, Hunter, Peters, Hunt, Charlton, Hurst.

England's Euro 68 Finals Squad   *Manager*: Sir Alf Ramsey

1	Gordon Banks	(Leicester City)	12	Alex Stepney	(Man Utd)
2	Keith Newton	(Blackburn)	13	Gordon West	(Everton)
3	Ray Wilson	(Everton)	14	Cyril Knowles	(Spurs)
4	Alan Mullery	(Spurs)	15	Jack Charlton	(Leeds Utd)
5	Brian Labone	(Everton)	16	Tommy Wright	(Everton)
6	Bobby Moore	(West Ham)	17	Nobby Stiles	(Man Utd)
7	Alan Ball	(Everton)	18	Mike Summerbee	(Man City)
8	Roger Hunt	(Liverpool)	19	Norman Hunter	(Leeds Utd)
9	Bobby Charlton	(Man Utd)	20	Colin Bell	(Man City)
10	Geoff Hurst	(West Ham)	21	Jimmy Greaves	(Spurs)
11	Martin Peters	(West Ham)	22	Peter Thompson	(Liverpool)

DID YOU KNOW THAT?

In 1968, UEFA renamed the "European Nations Cup" the "European Football Championship" with 31 teams entering the tournament. Up until 1976, only four teams entered the final tournament but from 1980 eight teams competed and then in 1996, 16 teams played in the final tournament. Germany has triumphed the most times, with three victories.

European Championship 1980

Having failed to qualify for the final stages of the 1972 and 1976 tournaments, England participated in their second European Championship finals in Italy in 1980. At the finals, England were drawn in Group 2 with Belgium, Spain and the hosts. England drew their opening game 1–1 with Belgium in the Stadio Communale, Turin on 12 June. Ray Wilkins gave England the lead midway through the first half, but Jan Ceulemans equalised soon after. A late goal from Italian midfielder Marco Tardelli gave the hosts a 1–0 win over England in Turin three days later. Goals from Trevor Brooking and Tony Woodcock were enough for England to beat Spain at the Stadio San Paolo, Naples, but they missed out a place in the last four. Belgium and Italy both collected a win and two draws to finish a point ahead of England, with Spain bottom of the group. The hosts advanced despite scoring only one goal in three matches, but they conceded none.

In the Final, Belgium faced West Germany. The Germans dominated the early exchanges and opened the scoring through Horst Hrubesch, who hit an unstoppable shot past Jean-Marie Pfaff. Late on in the game René van de Eycken equalised for the Belgians from the penalty spot, but just as extra-time loomed, Hrubesch scored again to give West Germany a 2–1 victory.

FIRST ROUND, GROUP 2

12 JUNE 1980, TURIN, 15,186

England (1) **1**   v   **Belgium** (1) **1**

(Wilkins 26)   (Ceulemans 30)

England: Clemence, Neal, Sansom, Watson, Thompson, Coppell (McDermott, 81), Wilkins, Brooking, Keegan, Johnson (Kennedy, 70), Woodcock.

15 JUNE 1980, TURIN, 59,649

Italy (0) **1**   **v**   **England** (0) **0**

(Tardelli 79)

England: Shilton, Neal, Sansom, Watson, Thompson,

Coppell, Wilkins, Kennedy, Keegan, Birtles (Mariner, 76), Woodcock.

18 JUNE 1980, NAPLES, 14,440

England (1) **2**   **v**   **Spain** (0) **1**

(Brooking 19, Woodcock 61)   (Dani pen 48)

England: Clemence, Anderson (Cherry, 83), Mills, Watson, Thompson, Wilkins,

Hoddle (Mariner, 76), Brooking, McDermott, Keegan, Woodcock.

GROUP 2 – FINAL TABLE

	P	W	D	L	F	A	Pts
Belgium	3	1	2	0	3	2	4
Italy	3	1	2	0	1	0	4
England	**3**	**1**	**1**	**1**	**3**	**3**	**3**
Spain	3	0	1	2	2	4	1

England's Euro 80 Finals Squad   *Manager*: Ron Greenwood

1	Ray Clemence	(Liverpool)	12	Viv Anderson	(Nottingham Forest)
2	Phil Neal	(Liverpool)	13	Peter Shilton	(Nottingham Forest)
3	Kenny Sansom	(Crystal Palace)	14	Trevor Cherry	(Leeds Utd)
4	Phil Thompson	(Liverpool)	15	Emlyn Hughes	(Wolves)
5	Dave Watson	(Southampton)	16	Mick Mills	(Ipswich Town)
6	Ray Wilkins	(Man Utd)	17	Terry McDermott	(Liverpool)
7	Kevin Keegan	(Hamburg SV)	18	Ray Kennedy	(Liverpool)
8	Steve Coppell	(Man Utd)	19	Glenn Hoddle	(Spurs)
9	David Johnson	(Liverpool)	20	Paul Mariner	(Ipswich Town)
10	Trevor Brooking	(West Ham)	21	Garry Birtles	(Nottingham Forest)
11	Tony Woodcock	(Arsenal)	22	Joe Corrigan	(Man City)

DID YOU KNOW THAT?

England didn't win another match in the European Championship finals until they beat Scotland 2–0 at Euro 96.

European Championship 1988

Having failed to qualify for the final stages of the 1984 tournament, England participated in their third European Championship finals in West Germany in 1988. England were drawn in Group 2 with Holland, the Republic of Ireland and the USSR. England had a torrid time, losing all three matches, and finished bottom of the group.

In their opening game at the Neckarstadion, Stuttgart, on 12 June, the Republic of Ireland beat Engalnd 1–0 with a goal from Ray Houghton. Three days later, a goal from Bryan Robson was overshadowed by a brilliant Marco van Basten hat-trick as Holland won 3–1 at the Rheinstadion, Düsseldorf. The final group match, against the Soviet Union at the Waldstadion, Frankfurt, also ended in a 3–1 defeat. Tony Adams scored England's goal.

Holland and the USSR went on to contest the Final in Munich, with the Dutch winning 2–0. Holland's Van Basten was voted the Player of the Tournament.

FIRST ROUND, GROUP 2

12 JUNE 1988, STUTTGART, 51,373

England (0) **0**   v   **Republic of Ireland** (1) **1**

(Houghton 6)

England: Shilton, Stevens G., Wright, Adams, Sansom, Waddle, Webb (Hoddle, 61), Robson, Barnes, Beardsley (Hateley, 81), Lineker.

15 JUNE 1988, DUSSELDORF, 63,940

England (0) **1**   v   **Holland** (1) **3**

(Robson 53)   (Van Basten 44, 71, 75)

England: Shilton, Stevens G., Wright, Adams, Sansom, Steven (Waddle, 69), Hoddle, Robson, Barnes, Beardsley (Hateley, 74), Lineker.

England (1) **1**   v   **Soviet Union** (2) **3**

(Adams 16)   (Aleinikov 3,

Mikhailichenko 28,

Pasulko 73)

England: Woods, Stevens G., Watson, Adams, Sansom, Steven, McMahon (Webb, 53), Robson, Hoddle, Lineker (Hateley, 64), Barnes.

GROUP 2 – FINAL TABLE

	P	W	D	L	F	A	Pts
Soviet Union	3	2	1	0	5	2	5
Holland	3	1	0	1	4	2	4
Rep of Ireland	3	1	1	1	2	2	3
England	**3**	**0**	**0**	**3**	**2**	**7**	**0**

England's Euro 88 Finals Squad   *Manager:* Bobby Robson

1	Peter Shilton	(Derby County)	11	John Barnes	(Liverpool)
2	Gary Stevens	(Everton)	12	Chris Waddle	(Spurs)
3	Kenny Sansom	(Arsenal)	13	Chris Woods	(Rangers)
4	Neil Webb	(Notts Forest)	14	Viv Anderson	(Man Utd)
5	Dave Watson	(Everton)	15	Steve McMahon	(Liverpool)
6	Tony Adams	(Arsenal)	16	Peter Reid	(Everton)
7	Bryan Robson	(Man Utd)	17	Glenn Hoddle	(AS Monaco)
8	Trevor Steven	(Everton)	18	Mark Hateley	(AS Monaco)
9	Peter Beardsley	(Liverpool)	19	Mark Wright	(Derby County)
10	Gary Lineker	(Barcelona)	20	Tony Dorigo	(Chelsea)

DID YOU KNOW THAT?

Holland, the country which gave the world "Total Football" in the 1970s, finally collected silverware at international level with their triumph at Euro 88. The team was coached by Rinus Michels, captained by Ruud Gullit and contained such stars as Ronald and Erwin Koeman, Arnold Muhren, Marco van Basten and Frank Rijkaard.

European Championship 1992

In 1992 England participated in their fourth European Championship finals, which were held in Sweden. At the finals, England were drawn in Group 1 with Denmark, France and the hosts, Sweden. It was another salutary experience for England, who went home bottom of the group and without winning a match.

England's first two games were at the Malmö Stadion and both ended in goalless draws, against Denmark and France, respectively. The last match was against Sweden at the Råsunda Stadion, Stockholm, and England knew a win would give them a semi-final place. David Platt scored after five minutes, but Jan Ericksson and Tomas Brolin replied in the second half to give Sweden a 2–1 victory, a result that left England bottom of the group with two points.

The surprise winners of the tournament were Denmark, last-minute replacements for the suspended Yugoslavia. They arrived with little time to prepare, and walked off with the trophy after beating Germany 2–0 in the Final in Gothenburg.

FIRST ROUND, GROUP 1

11 JUNE 1992, MALMO, 26,400

Denmark (0) **0**   v   **England** (0) **0**

England: Woods, Steven, Pearce, Curle (Daley, 62), Keown, Walker, Palmer, Platt, Merson (Webb, 71), Lineker, Smith.

14 JUNE 1992, MALMO, 26,500

France (0) **0**   v   **England** (0) **0**

England: Woods, Sinton, Pearce, Walker, Keown, Steven, Batty, Palmer, Platt, Shearer, Lineker.

Sweden (0) **2**   **v**   **England** (1) **1**

(Eriksson 54, Brolin 83)   (Platt 5)

England: Woods, Sinton (Merson, 77), Pearce, Keown,
Walker, Batty, Webb, Palmer, Platt, Daley, Lineker (Smith 65).

GROUP 1 – FINAL TABLE

	P	W	D	L	F	A	Pts
Sweden	3	2	1	0	4	2	5
Denmark	3	1	1	1	2	2	3
France	3	0	2	1	2	3	2
England	**3**	**0**	**2**	**1**	**1**	**2**	**2**

England's Euro 92 Finals Squad   *Manager:* Graham Taylor

1	Chris Woods	(Sheffield Wed)
2	Keith Curle	(Man City)
3	Stuart Pearce	(Nottm Forest)
4	Martin Keown	(Everton)
5	Des Walker	(Nottm Forest)
6	Mark Wright	(Liverpool)
7	David Platt	(Bari)
8	Trevor Steven	(Marseille)
9	Nigel Clough	(Nottm Forest)
10	Gary Lineker	(Spurs)
11	Andy Sinton	(QPR)
12	Carlton Palmer	(Sheffield Wed)

13	Nigel Martyn	(Crystal Palace)
14	Tony Dorigo	(Leeds United)
15	Neil Webb	(Man Utd)
16	Paul Merson	(Arsenal)
17	Alan Smith	(Arsenal)
18	Tony Daley	(Aston Villa)
19	David Batty	(Leeds Utd)
20	Alan Shearer	(Southampton)

John Barnes (Liverpool), Lee Dixon (Arsenal) and Gary Stevens (Rangers) withdrew from the squad because of injuries.

DID YOU KNOW THAT?

It was during the Sweden defeat that the England manager, Graham Taylor, uttered the famous words "Do I not like that" just before Tomas Brolin scored what proved to be Sweden's match-winning goal. If England had equalised they would have finished with the same points and goals (for and against) as Denmark.

European Championship 1996

England hosted Euro 96 and were in Group A with Holland, Switzerland and Scotland. In their opening game, England drew 1–1 with the Swiss. England won their next two matches, 2–0 over Scotland and 4–1 against Holland to finish top of the group. In the quarter-finals, England beat Spain 4–2 in a penalty shoot-out after 120 goalless minutes. The semi-final, against Germany, also required penalties, this time after a 1–1 draw, but Germany won 6–5.

Germany went on to win the Final against the Czech Republic, 2–1, on a golden goal from Oliver Bierhoff.

FIRST ROUND, GROUP A

8 JUNE 1996, WEMBLEY, 76,567

England (1) **1** v **Switzerland** (0) **1**

(Shearer 23)   (Turkylmaz 84)

England: Seaman, Neville, G., Pearce, Adams, Southgate, Anderton, Gascoigne (Platt, 77), McManaman (Stone, 67), Sheringham (Barmby, 67), Shearer.

15 JUNE 1996, WEMBLEY, 77,000

England (1) **2** v **Scotland** (0) **0**

(Shearer 53, Gascoigne 79)

England: Seaman, Neville, G., Pearce (Redknapp, 46 [Campbell, 85]) Adams, Southgate, Ince (Stone, 80), Anderton, Gascoigne, McManaman, Sheringham, Shearer.

18 JUNE 1996, WEMBLEY, 76,798

England (1) **4** v **Holland** (0) **1**

(Shearer 23, 57,   (Kluivert 78)

Sheringham 51, 62)

England: Seaman, Neville, G., Pearce, Adams, Southgate, Ince (Platt, 67), McManaman, Gascoigne, Anderton, Sheringham (Fowler, 75), Shearer (Barmby, 75).

	P	W	D	L	F	A	Pts
England	**3**	**2**	**1**	**0**	**7**	**2**	**7**
Holland	3	1	1	1	3	4	4
Scotland	3	1	1	1	1	2	4
Switzerland	3	0	1	2	1	4	1

QUARTER-FINAL

22 JUNE 1996, WEMBLEY, 75,440

England (0) **0**   v   **Spain** (0) **0**

England won 4–2 on penalties after extra-time

England: Seaman, Neville, G., Pearce, Adams, Southgate, McManaman (Stone,

109), Platt, Gascoigne, Anderton (Barmby, 109), Sheringham (Fowler, 109), Shearer.

SEMI-FINAL

26 JUNE 1996, WEMBLEY, 75,862

England (1) **1**   v   **Germany** (1) **1**

(Shearer 3)   (Kuntz 16)

Germany won 6–5 on penalties after extra-time

England: Seaman, Ince, Pearce, Adams, Southgate, McManaman,

Platt, Gascoigne, Anderton, Sheringham, Shearer.

England's Euro 96 Finals Squad   *Manager:* Terry Venables

1	David Seaman	(Arsenal)	12	Steve Howey	(Newcastle Utd)
2	Gary Neville	(Man Utd)	13	Tim Flowers	(Blackburn)
3	Stuart Pearce	(Nottm Forest)	14	Nicky Barmby	(Middlesbrough)
4	Paul Ince	(Inter Milan)	15	Jamie Redknapp	(Liverpool)
5	Tony Adams	(Arsenal)	16	Sol Campbell	(Spurs)
6	Gareth Southgate	(Aston Villa)	17	Steve McManaman	(Liverpool)
7	David Platt	(Arsenal)	18	Les Ferdinand	(Newcastle Utd)
8	Paul Gascoigne	(Rangers)	19	Philip Neville	(Man Utd)
9	Alan Shearer	(Blackburn)	20	Steve Stone	(Nottm Forest)
10	Teddy Sheringham	(Spurs)	21	Robbie Fowler	(Liverpool)
11	Darren Anderton	(Spurs)	22	Ian Walker	(Spurs)

European Championship 2000

In 2000, England participated in their sixth European Championship finals, which were co-hosted by Belgium and the Netherlands. At the finals, England were drawn in Group A with Germany, Portugal and Romania.

England lost their opening match 3–2 to Portugal, despite leading 2–0 after 18 minutes, in the Phillips Stadion, Eindhoven, Netherlands. Germany, the holders, were England's next opponents and England gained revenge for their semi-final penalty shoot-out defeat of four years earlier with a 1–0 win in the Stade Communal, Charleroi, Belgium, thanks to an Alan Shearer goal. In their final group game, England lost 3–2 to the Romanians in the Stade Communal, Charleroi, Belgium, a result that left England third in the group and out of the competition.

France beat Italy 2–1 in the Final in Rotterdam with a golden goal from David Trezeguet in extra time.

FIRST ROUND, GROUP A

12 JUNE 2000, EINDHOVEN, 31,500

Portugal (2) **3**   v   **England** (2) **2**

(Figo 22, João Pinto 37,   (Scholes 3,

Gomes 59)   McManaman 18)

England: Seaman, Neville G., Neville P., Campbell, Adams (Keown, 82), Beckham, Scholes, Ince, McManaman (Wise, 58), Shearer, Owen (Heskey, 46).

17 JUNE 2000, CHARLEROI, 27,700

Germany (0) **0**   v   **England** (0) **1**

(Shearer 53)

England: Seaman, Neville G., Neville P., Campbell, Keown, Beckham, Scholes (Barmby, 71), Ince, Wise, Shearer, Owen (Gerrard, 61).

England (2) **2**   **v**   **Romania** (1) **3**

(Shearer 41, Owen 45)   (Chivu 22, Munteanu 48,

Ganea pen 89)

England: Martyn, Neville G., Neville P., Campbell, Keown, Beckham, Scholes

(Southgate, 82), Ince, Wise (Barmby, 75), Shearer, Owen (Heskey, 67).

GROUP A – FINAL TABLE

	P	W	D	L	F	A	Pts
Portugal	3	3	0	0	7	2	9
Romania	3	1	1	1	4	4	4
England	**3**	**1**	**0**	**2**	**5**	**6**	**3**
Germany	3	0	1	2	1	5	1

England's Euro 2000 Finals Squad   *Manager*: Kevin Keegan

1	David Seaman	(Arsenal)	12	Gareth Southgate	(Aston Villa)
2	Gary Neville	(Man Utd)	13	Nigel Martyn	(Leeds United)
3	Phil Neville	(Man Utd)	14	Paul Ince	(Middlesbrough)
4	Sol Campbell	(Spurs)	15	Gareth Barry	(Aston Villa)
5	Tony Adams	(Arsenal)	16	Steven Gerrard	(Liverpool)
6	Martin Keown	(Arsenal)	17	Dennis Wise	(Chelsea)
7	David Beckham	(Man Utd)	18	Nicky Barmby	(Everton)
8	Paul Scholes	(Man Utd)	19	Emile Heskey	(Liverpool)
9	Alan Shearer	(Newcastle Utd)	20	Kevin Phillips	(Sunderland)
10	Michael Owen	(Liverpool)	21	Robbie Fowler	(Liverpool)
11	Steve McManaman	(R Madrid)	22	Richard Wright	(Ipswich Town)

DID YOU KNOW THAT?

UEFA seeded four teams to head the four groups: Belgium and Netherlands as the co-host nations, Germany as the reigning European Champions, and Spain as the highest-placed team in UEFA's European national team ranking. England were ranked 17th in Europe and were placed among those teams that were seeded fourth and lowest.

European Championship 2004

The 2004 European Championship finals were held in Portugal. At the finals, England were drawn in Group B with Croatia, France and Switzerland. England lost their opening game to France 2–1 in the Estádio da Luz, Lisbon, beat the Swiss 3–0 in the Estádio Municipal de Coimbra, and beat Croatia 4–2 in the Estádio da Luz. England finished second to France in the group and progressed to the quarter-finals where they drew 2–2 with Portugal, Frank Lampard and Michael Owen scoring, before going out of the competition in a penalty shoot-out, losing 6–5.

Greece joined Denmark in becoming shock winners of the European Championship when they beat hosts Portugal in the Final in Lisbon. Defending solidly and counter-attacking dangerously, they scored the only goal of the game through Angelos Charisteas after 56 minutes.

FIRST ROUND, GROUP B

13 JUNE 2004, LISBON, 65,200

France (0) **2**   v   **England** (1) **1**

(Zidane 90, 90)   (Lampard 39)

England: James, Neville G., Cole, Campbell, King, Beckham, Lampard, Gerrard, Scholes (Hargreaves, 76), Owen (Vassell, 69), Rooney (Heskey, 76).

17 JUNE 2004, COIMBRA, 28,500

England (1) **3**   v   **Switzerland** (0) **0**

(Rooney 23, 76,
Gerrard 83)

England: James, Neville G., Cole, Terry, Campbell, Beckham, Gerrard, Lampard, Scholes (Hargreaves, 71), Owen (Vassell, 73), Rooney (Dyer, 84).

21 JUNE 2004, LISBON, 57,047

Croatia (1) **2**   v   **England** (2) **4**

(Kovac N. 5, Tudor 73)   (Scholes 40, Rooney 46, 67,

Lampard 78)

England: James, Neville G., Cole, Campbell, Terry, Beckham, Gerrard, Scholes

(King, 69), Lampard (Neville P., 83), Owen, Rooney (Vassell, 71).

GROUP B – FINAL TABLE

	P	W	D	L	F	A	Pts
France	3	2	1	0	7	4	7
England	**3**	**2**	**0**	**1**	**8**	**4**	**6**
Croatia	3	0	2	1	4	6	2
Switzerland	3	0	1	2	1	6	1

QUARTER-FINAL

24 JUNE 2004, LISBON, 62,564

Portugal (0) **2**   v   **England** (1) **2**

(Postiga 83, Rui Costa 110)   (Owen 3, Lampard 115)

England lost 5–6 on penalties after extra-time (90min: 1–1)

England: James, Neville G., Cole, Campbell, Terry, Beckham, Gerrard

(Hargreaves, 81), Scholes (Neville P., 57), Lampard, Owen, Rooney (Vassell, 27).

England's Euro 2004 Finals Squad   *Manager*: Sven-Goran Eriksson

1	David James	(Man City)	13	Paul Robinson	(Spurs)
2	Gary Neville	(Man Utd)	14	Phil Neville	(Man Utd)
3	Ashley Cole	(Arsenal)	15	Ledley King	(Spurs)
4	Steven Gerrard	(Liverpool)	16	Jamie Carragher	(Liverpool)
5	John Terry	(Chelsea)	17	Nicky Butt	(Man Utd)
6	Sol Campbell	(Arsenal)	18	Owen Hargreaves	(B Munich)
7	David Beckham	(R Madrid)	19	Joe Cole	(Chelsea)
8	Paul Scholes	(Man Utd)	20	Kieron Dyer	(Newcastle Utd)
9	Wayne Rooney	(Man Utd)	21	Emile Heskey	(Liverpool)
10	Michael Owen	(Liverpool)	22	Ian Walker	(Leicester City)
11	Frank Lampard	(Chelsea)	23	Darius Vassell	(Aston Villa)
12	Wayne Bridge	(Chelsea)			

European Championship 2008

England found themselves in Group E of the 2008 European Championship qualifying competition, facing six rivals, the most difficult of which seemed to be Croatia and Russia. New coach Steve McClaren had a gentle introduction to competitive internationals with Andorra providing scant opposition at Old Trafford, Manchester. Two goals each from Peter Crouch and Jermain Defoe, plus one from Steven Gerrard gave England a comfortable 5–0 victory.

Crouch was again on target in the next match, and it was enough to see off the Former Yugoslav Republic of Macedonia in Skopje. But the first alarm bells rang when the return at Wembley ended in a goalless draw. Worse was to follow when England lost 2–0 in Croatia, with Gary Neville scoring a freak own goal. A 0–0 away draw to Israel left England with eight points from five matches. They had to turn things around in a hurry, but they did so in style, with five straight 3–0 wins, in Andorra and Estonia, then at home to Israel, Russia and Estonia, the result against the Russians seeming to all but confirm England's qualification.

But it all went wrong in the final two matches. England's penultimate match was on the artificial turf at the Luzhniki Stadium, Moscow, and despite a first-half Wayne Rooney goal, two in reply from Roman Pavlyuchenko, one a penalty, meant that Russia won 2–1.

England did not play on the penultimate match-day and although Croatia booked their finals place, England lay second in the group, two points ahead of Russia and with a much better – plus-8 – goal difference. England thus needed only a draw against Croatia to qualify.

But on a rain-soaked night at Wembley, England fell behind 2–0 in the first 15 minutes and although Frank Lampard and Crouch brought England level, a late long-range effort from substitute Mladen Petric gave Croatia a 3–2 victory, with Russia claiming the second qualifying place with a 1–0 win in Andorra. Crouch was England's leading scorer in the group, with five goals.

England's results in Group E were as follows:

Date	Opponent	Venue	Res	Score	England scorers
2/9/06	Andorra	Manchester	W	5–0	Crouch 5, 66, Gerrard 13, Defoe 38, 47
6/9/06	Macedonia	Skopje	W	1–0	Crouch 46
7/10/06	Macedonia	Wembley	D	0–0	
11/10/06	Croatia	Zagreb	L	0–2	
24/3/07	Israel	Tel Aviv	D	0–0	
28/3/07	Andorra	Barcelona	W	3–0	Gerrard 54, 76, Nugent 90
6/6/07	Estonia	Tallinn	W	3–0	J. Cole 37, Crouch 54, Owen 62
8/9/07	Israel	Wembley	W	3–0	Wright-Phillips 20, Owen 49, Richards 66
12/9/07	Russia	Wembley	W	3–0	Owen 7, 31, Ferdinand 84
13/10/07	Estonia	Wembley	W	3–0	Wright-Phillips 11, Rooney 32, Rahn (og) 32
17/10/07	Russia	Moscow	L	1–2	Rooney 29
21/11/07	Croatia	Wembley	L	2–3	Lampard pen 56, Crouch 65

GROUP E – FINAL TABLE

	P	W	D	L	F	A	Pts
Croatia	12	9	2	1	28	8	29
Russia	12	7	3	2	18	7	24
England	**12**	**7**	**2**	**3**	**24**	**7**	**23**
Israel	12	7	2	3	20	12	23
FYR Macedonia	12	4	2	6	12	12	14
Estonia	12	2	1	9	5	21	7
Andorra	12	0	0	12	2	42	0

DID YOU KNOW THAT?

As England lost in the rain to Croatia, coach Steve McClaren watched on holding a giant umbrella. The tabloid media wasted no time in dubbing him "The Wally with the brolly".

CHAPTER

4

ENGLAND
FANTASY TEAMS

There is no better way to while away a wet Wednesday at Wembley by dreaming that you are the England coach and you can pick the team. Of course, as you support one particular club you will select only players from that club. So here it is, a selection of fantasy England teams, all picked from just one club (and, for variety, one made up from only those men honoured to wear the captain's armband).

This chapter is sure to get you shouting in frustration at the fantasy teams selected, because you know you can do better, especially as your favourite player isn't in the squad. The beauty of these fantasy teams is that we are not wrong, nor are you. As the proverb goes, "one man's meat is another man's poison", or in this case, "one man's legend is another man's donkey".

For almost 90 years it was believed that fantasy and reality had collided in the 1880s when England twice faced Wales with a team comprising players from only one club – the legendary Corinthians. Sadly, this is just fantasy because although all 11 players had played for Corinthians, many were officially attached to other clubs at the time.

Arsenal England XI

1
David *SEAMAN*

2
Lee *DIXON*

6
Martin *KEOWN*

5
Tony *ADAMS*

3
Ashley *COLE*

7
Theo *WALCOTT*

8
David *PLATT*

4
Alan *BALL*

11
Paul *MERSON*

9
Ian *WRIGHT*

10
Charlie *GEORGE*

Substitutes

Richard **WRIGHT,** Ray **PARLOUR,** Steve **BOULD,**

Nigel **WINTERBURN,** Cliff **BASTIN**

Manager

Joe **MERCER**

DID YOU KNOW THAT?

Arsenal were founded as Dial Square in 1886 by factory workers at the Royal Arsenal in Woolwich, London, and were then renamed Royal Arsenal shortly afterwards. When the club turned professional in 1891, there was a further name change, to Woolwich Arsenal. In 1913, the club relocated to North London, near to the Gillespie Road Underground station. As it was miles from Woolwich, the club dropped the suburb and became simply Arsenal. In the 1930s London Underground changed Gillespie Road station to Arsenal.

Aston Villa England XI

1
Sam *HARDY*

2
Howard *SPENCER*

6
Gareth *SOUTHGATE*

5
Ugo *EHIOGU*

3
Gareth *BARRY*

7
Tony *DALEY*

8
Steve *STONE*

4
Frank *BARSON*

11
Gordon *COWANS*

9
Peter *WITHE*

10
William *WALKER*

Substitutes

David *JAMES,* Earl *BARRETT,* Lee *HENDRIE,*
Paul *MERSON,* Darius *VASSELL*

Manager

Graham *TAYLOR*

DID YOU KNOW THAT?

The club was formed in 1874 as the Cricketers of Villa Cross Wesleyan Church. Villa's first match was against Aston Brook St Mary's rugby side and, as a condition of the match, they agreed to play the first half under the laws of rugby and the second half under association football rules. Villa sneaked a 1–0 victory. Aston Villa moved to Villa Park in 1897 and the stadium has hosted more FA Cup semi-final matches, 55, than any other. England's first full international at Villa Park was in 1899, the 16th and most recent, was in 2005.

Chelsea England XI

1
Peter
BONETTI

2
Glen
JOHNSON

6
John
TERRY

5
John
HOLLINS

3
Ashley
COLE

7
Dennis
WISE

8
Frank
LAMPARD

4
Ray
WILKINS

11
Joe
COLE

9
Jimmy
GREAVES

10
Bobby
TAMBLING

Substitutes

Dave ***BEASANT,*** Graeme ***LE SAUX,*** Terry ***VENABLES,***

Peter ***OSGOOD,*** Kerry ***DIXON***

Manager

Glenn ***HODDLE***

DID YOU KNOW THAT?

Chelsea Football Club was founded in 1905 and they were elected straight into the Football League after the Southern League rejected them. The club nickname is the Blues, but they were previously known as the Pensioners, after the famous Royal Hospital. Despite its old nickname, the club's Stamford Bridge ground is actually situated just outside the Royal Borough of Kensington and Chelsea; the border is the railway line running behind the main stand. Their ground is on the Fulham Road in Hammersmith and Fulham.

Leeds United England XI

1
Nigel
MARTYN

2
Paul
REANEY

6
Jack
CHARLTON

5
Norman
HUNTER

3
Tony
DORIGO

7
David
BATTY

8
Paul
MADELEY

4
Tony
CURRIE

11
Mike
O'GRADY

9
Allan
CLARKE

10
Mick
JONES

Substitutes

Paul **ROBINSON,** Terry **COOPER,** Trevor **CHERRY,**

Rio **FERDINAND,** Alan **SMITH**

Manager

Don **REVIE**

DID YOU KNOW THAT?

Leeds United's predecessor club, Leeds City FC, was formed in 1904 before it was disbanded in 1919 by the Football Association after financial irregularities. From the old club Leeds United AFC was formed and turned professional in 1920, taking the place of Leeds City's reserve side in the Midland League. Leeds' manager at the time was Herbert Chapman, and he later assembled both the Huddersfield Town and Arsenal teams which won three consecutive League championships in the 1920s and 1930s.

Liverpool England XI

1
Ray
CLEMENCE

2
Phil
NEAL

6
Tommy
SMITH

5
Phil
THOMPSON

3
Alec
LINDSAY

7
Emlyn
HUGHES

8
Kevin
KEEGAN

4
Steven
GERRARD

11
John
BARNES

9
Michael
OWEN

10
Robbie
FOWLER

Substitutes

David *JAMES*, Jamie *CARRAGHER*, Larry *LLOYD*,

Emile *HESKEY*, Ian *CALLAGHAN*

Player-Manager

Kevin *KEEGAN*

DID YOU KNOW THAT?

The first Football League club in the city of Liverpool was Everton, and they played their home games at Anfield. The Blues, however, fell out with John Houlding, the owner of the Anfield stadium, over a proposed rent increase for the 1892–93 season, so they moved across Stanley Park to Goodison Park. Houlding, meanwhile, decided to form a new club to play at his stadium and Liverpool FC was born. They were elected straight into the Football League in 1893.

Manchester United England XI

1
Alex
STEPNEY

2
Gary
NEVILLE

6
Charlie
ROBERTS

5
Rio
FERDINAND

3
Roger
BYRNE

7
Duncan
EDWARDS

8
Bryan
ROBSON

4
Paul
SCHOLES

11
Bobby
CHARLTON

9
Tommy
TAYLOR

10
Wayne
ROONEY

Substitutes

Gary **BAILEY**, Paul **PARKER**, Ray **WILKINS**,

Steve **COPPELL**, Jack **ROWLEY**

Manager

Walter **WINTERBOTTOM**

DID YOU KNOW THAT?

Manchester United began life as Newton Heath in 1878 when a group of workers from the Lancashire & Yorkshire Railways formed a football team. Newton Heath takes its name from the old English meaning "the new town on the heath". In the early days the players used the nearby pub, the Three Crowns Inn, for changing facilities. When Newton Heath moved to Bank Street, they changed their name to Manchester United. The move to Old Trafford came in 1910.

Newcastle United England XI

1
Matthew
KINGSLEY

2
John
CARR

6
Jonathan
WOODGATE

5
Francis
HUDSPETH

3
David
BATTY

7
Paul
GASCOIGNE

8
Kevin
KEEGAN

4
Peter
BEARDSLEY

11
Chris
WADDLE

9
Alan
SHEARER

10
Jackie
MILBURN

Substitutes

Warren **BARTON,** Steve **HOWEY,** Jonathan **WOODGATE,**

Les **FERDINAND,** Michael **OWEN**

Manager

Sir Bobby **ROBSON, CBE**

DID YOU KNOW THAT?

Newcastle United began life as Newcastle East End from 1882–92. When Newcastle West End was wound up in 1892, some of its players and most of its backroom staff joined East End. East End also took over the lease on St James's Park and in December 1892, East End became Newcastle United. In November 2009, there was furore on Tyneside when the club's owner, Mike Ashley, who had just presided over the Magpies' relegation from the Premier League, said he was looking to sell the naming rights to St James's Park.

Sheffield Wednesday England XI

1
Chris
WOODS

2
Mel
STERLAND

6
Des
WALKER

5
Peter
SWAN

3
Andy
HINCHCLIFFE

7
Chris
WADDLE

8
Jackie
SEWELL

4
Carlton
PALMER

11
Albert
QUIXALL

9
David
HIRST

10
Fred
SPIKSLEY

Substitutes

Ron *SPRINGETT,* John *FANTHAM,* John *ROBINSON,*

Gerry *YOUNG,* Ronnie *STARLING*

Manager

Howard *WILKINSON*

DID YOU KNOW THAT?

The club was formed on 4 September 1867 and was, in the beginning, a cricket team, with football being played during the winter to keep the team together. Sheffield Wednesday turned professional in 1887 and were elected to the First Division of the Football League in 1892. The club's nickname is the Owls, taken from the name of the borough in which they play, Owlerton (but it is pronounced Ollerton). Hillsborough, the name of the ground, is taken from the parliamentary constituency in which it lies.

Southampton England XI

1
Peter
SHILTON

2
Alf
RAMSEY

6
Dave
WATSON

5
Mark
WRIGHT

3
Mick
MILLS

7
Terry
PAINE

8
Kevin
KEEGAN

4
Matt
LE TISSIER

11
Steve
WILLIAMS

9
Alan
SHEARER

10
Mick
CHANNON

Substitutes

Tim *FLOWERS,* Graeme *LE SAUX,* Jamie *REDKNAPP,*

Kevin *PHILIPS,* Peter *CROUCH*

Player-Manager

Sir *ALF RAMSEY*

DID YOU KNOW THAT?

Southampton Football Club began life as St Mary's YMA. The Saints were formed in November 1885 and occupied the Dell for over 100 years before moving to its existing St Mary's Stadium in 2001. Southampton's greatest day came in the 1976 FA Cup Final when they beat Manchester United 1–0. The Saints had a reputation for loyalty. Between 1955 and 1985, they had only two managers, Ted Bates and Lawrie McMenemy. In addition players Terry Paine and Matt Le Tissier were at Southampton for 18 and 16 years, respectively.

Tottenham Hotspur England XI

1
Ray
CLEMENCE

2
Alf
RAMSEY

6
Sol
CAMPBELL

5
Gary
MABBUTT

3
Cyril
KNOWLES

4
Allan
MULLERY

8
Glenn
HODDLE

11
Paul
GASCOIGNE

7
Chris
WADDLE

9
Jimmy
GREAVES

10
Gary
LINEKER

Substitutes

Ian *WALKER,* Ledley *KING,* Steve *PERRYMAN,*

Martin *CHIVERS,* Teddy *SHERINGHAM*

Manager

Terry *VENABLES*

DID YOU KNOW THAT?

Tottenham Hotspur were one of only three teams in the 20th century to win the FA Cup in consecutive years and the only side to have done so on two occasions. Spurs first won the FA Cup in 1901, before they were in the Football League. They were the first club to complete the double of Football League Championship and victory in the FA Cup Final in the 20th century and the first British club to win a European trophy when they claimed the European Cup-Winners' Cup in 1963.

West Ham United England XI

Substitutes

Paul *KONCHESKY*, Alvin *MARTIN*, Joe *COLE*,

Teddy *SHERINGHAM*, Tony *COTTEE*

Manager

Ron *GREENWOOD*

DID YOU KNOW THAT?

The club was founded in 1895 as the works' team from the Thames Ironworks and Shipbuilding Co. Ltd. In 1899, the club joined the Southern League Division Two and in 1900, became a limited company and changed its name to West Ham United. They did not become members of the Football League until 1919, but the club played in the first FA Cup Final at Wembley Stadium in 1923, losing 2–0 to Bolton Wanderers. The club has two nicknames: the Irons, from the original club; and the Hammers, from the present-day one.

Captains England XI

1
Peter
SHILTON
(15)

2
Phil
NEAL
(1)

6
Bobby
MOORE
(90)

5
Billy
WRIGHT
(90)

3
Mick
MILLS
(8)

7
Bryan
ROBSON
(65)

8
Ray
WILKINS
(10)

4
Bobby
CHARLTON
(3)

11
Martin
PETERS
(4)

9
Gary
LINEKER
(18)

10
Kevin
KEEGAN
(31)

Substitutes

Ray **CLEMENCE (1)**, Trevor **CHERRY (1)**, Emlyn **HUGHES (23)**,
Gerry **FRANCIS (8)**, Alan **BALL (6)**, David **BECKHAM (59)**, Alan **SHEARER (34)**

Manager

ALF RAMSEY (3)

Number of times the player captained England in parenthesis.

DID YOU KNOW THAT?

England have been led by 108 captains in their 881 matches since the first international in 1872, up to the Brazil match on 14 November 2009. Bobby Moore and Billy Wright, the first two men to reach 100 international caps, both led England 90 times, while both Bryan Robson and David Beckham have led out the team on more than 50 occasions. Fabio Capello's first regular skipper, John Terry, wore the armband 28 times in 58 appearances up to the end of 2009.

CHAPTER

5

NATIONAL PRIDE: England captain Bobby Moore holds aloft the Jules Rimet trophy after the dramatic 4–2 extra-time defeat of West Germany in the 1966 World Cup Final at Wembley Stadium.

DIVINE INTERVENTION: Diego Maradona's infamous "Hand of God" goal which helped knock England out of the 1986 World Cup Finals in Mexico.

LUCK OF THE IRISH: Gary Lineker scores for England against the Republic of Ireland in their opening Group F game in Cagliari during the Italia 90 World Cup.

GAZZA'S TEARS: An emotional Paul Gascoigne weeps after England's 1990 World Cup semi-final penalty shoot-out loss to West Germany. He would have missed the Final.

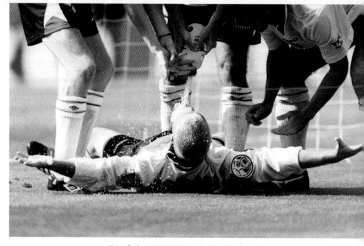

COLD SHOWER: Paul Gascoigne is squirted with water by team-mates in the famous "dentist's chair" celebration of his superb goal against Scotland in Euro 96 at Wembley.

COME ON! England hardman Stuart Pearce banishes the nightmare of his Italy 90 semi-final penalty miss against West Germany with a successful attempt in the 4–2 shoot-out win over Spain in England's Euro 96 quarter-final at Wembley.

A NIGHT TO REMEMBER: The Munich scoreboard records England's 5–1 rout of Germany in the qualifying tournament for the 2002 World Cup finals.

SWEET REVENGE: On 7 June 2002, nearly four years after his red card at France 98, David Beckham celebrates as his penalty gives England the lead against Argentina in Sapporo.

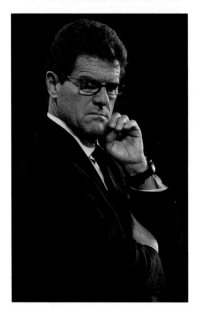

SERGEANT CAPELLO: England coach Fabio Capello is nicknamed "The Iron Sergeant."

WAYNE'S WORLD: England's Wayne Rooney – Europe's leading goalscorer in qualifying for the 2010 World Cup – attempts a spectacular volley against Kazakhstan in October 2008.

GOLDEN BALLS: England's former skipper and most capped outfield player David Beckham applauds the fans.

BAFANA! BAFANA! Wayne Rooney is mobbed by his team-mates after scoring the last goal in the 5–1 victory over Croatia in the World Cup qualifier at Wembley in September 2009 that clinched England's place at the finals of the 2010 World Cup.

ENGLAND LISTS & TRIVIA

If you love facts and stats in easy-to-digest chunks, then this is the section for you. Every important tidbit of England information will be found in the next few pages, in simple tabular format, whether it is the most capped players and leading goalscorers, or managers/ coaches or penalties faced by goalkeepers.

In addition to these top 10s, there are some other nuggets of information to expand your knowledge and make you look a complete genius in the eyes of friends and colleagues. Study these lists carefully and you will be able tell everyone who scored the fastest ever goal for England, against whom, where and when.

And if that isn't enough, you will find other fantastic stuff, such as the names of all the brothers who have played for England, either together or separately, weird and wonderful nicknames, the 52 grounds on which England have played home matches (it's 53 if you count the old and new versions of Wembley Stadium separately), 57 nations to face England at Wembley and all the men to have led their country into football battle, as it were.

In these days of information overload, you can learn which stars have written autobiographies and which are stars of the big and small screens.

England's Band of Brothers

Twenty sets of brothers have played full internationals for England.

Bambridge, Arthur *(3 caps, 1879–74, Swifts, Corinthians),* Charles *(18, 1879–87, Swifts, Corinthians)* and Ernest *(1, 1876, Swifts)* • **Charlton,** Jack *(35 caps, 1965–70, Leeds)* and Bobby *(106, 1958–70, Man Utd)* • **Clegg,** Charles *(1 cap, 1872, Wednesday)* and William *(2, 1873–79, Wednesday, Sheffield Albion)* • **Corbett,** Bert *(1 cap, 1901 Corinthians)* and Reg *(1, 1903, Old Malvernians)* • **Cursham,** Arthur *(6 caps, 1876–83, Notts County)* and Henry *(8, 1880–84, Notts County)* • **Dobson,** Alfred *(4 caps, Notts County, 1882–84)* and Charles *(1, 1886, Notts County)* • **Forman,** Frank *(9 caps, 1898–1903 Nottingham Forest)* and Fred *(3, 1899, Nottingham Forest)* • **Hargreaves,** Fred *(3 caps, 1880–82, Blackburn Rovers)* and John *(2, 1881, Blackburn Rovers)* • **Heron,** Francis *(1 cap 1876, Wanderers)* and Hubert *(5, 1873–78, Uxbridge, Wanderers)* • **Lyttelton,** Alfred *(1 cap, 1877, Cambridge Univ)* and Edward *(1, 1878, Cambridge Univ)* • **Neville,** Gary *(80 caps, 1995–present, Man Utd)* and Philip *(36, 1996–present, Man Utd, Everton)* • **Osborne,** Frank *(4 caps, 1923–26, Fulham, Spurs)* and Reg *(1, 1928, Leicester City)* • **Perry,** Charles *(3 caps, 1890–93, WBA)* and Thomas *(1, 1898, WBA)* • **Rawson,** Herbert *(1 cap, 1875, Royal Engineers)* and William *(2, 1875–77, Oxford Univ)* • **Shelton,** Alf *(6 caps, 1889–92, Notts County)* and Charles *(1, 1888, Notts Rangers)* • **Smith,** John *(3 caps, 1931, Portsmouth)* and Septimus *(1, 1935, Leicester City)* • **Stephenson,** Clem *(1 cap, 1924, Huddersfield Town)* and George *(1928–31, Derby Co, Sheffield Wednesday)* • **Topham,** Arthur *(1 cap, 1894, Casuals)* and Robert *(2, 1893–94, Wolves, Casuals)* • **Walters,** Arthur *(9 caps, 1885–90, Cambridge Univ, Old Carthusians)* and Percy *(13, 1885–90, Oxford Univ, Old Carthusians)* • **Wilson,** Charles *(1 cap, 1884, Hendon)* and Geoffrey *(2, 1900, Corinthians)*

The Battle of Highbury

In 1934 England and Italy were regarded by many as the two best teams in the world. England fielded seven Arsenal players for this friendly as it was played at their club ground, Highbury. Early in the game an Italian player was taken off injured and, with no substitutes permitted in those days, they had to play the rest of the game a man short. Italy set about England and turned the first half into a war. Several of the home players were badly injured, one suffering a broken arm and another a broken nose.

A crowd of more than 56,000 watched on as England took the lead after eight minutes through Manchester City's left-winger Eric Brook and the same player doubled the advantage just two minutes later. After a quarter of an hour Ted Drake added a third goal for England and it stayed 3–0 until half-time.

The second half was not as violent as the first and a more subdued Italy pulled two goals back, both scored by Giuseppi Meazza, after 58 and 62 minutes. Many of the England players claimed it was the dirtiest game they'd ever played in – hence it became known in football folklore as "The Battle of Highbury".

England: Moss, Male, Hapgood, Britton, Barker, Copping, Matthews, Bowden, Drake, Bastin, Brook.

DID YOU KNOW THAT?
Arsenal team-mates right-back George Male and centre-forward Ted Drake both made their debuts in this match, while it was the last time goalkeeper Frank Moss pulled on an England shirt.

England's Nine World Cup Captains

Only nine players have led England in World Cup finals. England were led by their first-choice captains Billy Wright in 1950, 1954 and 1958, Johnny Haynes in 1962, and Bobby Moore in 1966 and 1970. Mick Mills was captain for the 1982 finals as a result of Kevin Keegan's injury, although Keegan did come on as a substitute in England's final match.

Bryan Robson was the England captain for both the 1986 and 1990 finals but injuries in both tournaments restricted his appearances. In 1986 in Mexico, a shoulder injury forced off Robson in the first half of England's second group game, against Morocco, and he did not play any further part in the tournament. Ray Wilkins took over the captain's armband, but after he was sent off soon after Robson's injury he handed the armband to Peter Shilton, who then captained England in their wins over Poland and Paraguay, and in the loss to Argentina. When injury forced Robson's withdrawal in the second group match against Holland at the 1990 finals in Italy, Shilton and Terry Butcher both filled in as captain. Shilton was captain for the two matches in which Butcher did not play: the third group match against Egypt and the third-place play-off game against Italy. Butcher had the armband against Belgium, Cameroon and West Germany.

At France in 1998, Alan Shearer was captain in all four England games. In 2002 and 2006 David Beckham was Sven-Goran Eriksson's choice as team leader, captaining the team in all 10 games. When he was substituted in the opening game with Sweden in 2002, Michael Owen took the armband. And when Beckham was injured in the 2006 quarter-final against Portugal, Gary Neville led the team.

Rio Ferdinand is likely to be captain in South Africa 2010.

England Honours List

KNIGHTHOODS

Name	Year	Name	Year
John Charles Clegg	1927	Tom Finney	1998
Stanley Matthews	1965	Geoff Hurst	1998
Alf Ramsey	1967	Bobby Robson	2002
Walter Winterbottom	1978	Trevor Brooking	2004
Bobby Charlton	1994		

COMMANDERS OF THE ORDER OF THE BRITISH EMPIRE (CBE)

Stanley Matthews	1957	Bobby Robson	1990
Billy Wright	1959	Tom Finney	1992
Walter Winterbottom	1972	Trevor Brooking	1999
Bobby Charlton	1974	Steven Gerrard	2007
Ron Greenwood	1983		

OFFICERS OF THE ORDER OF THE BRITISH EMPIRE (OBE)

Tom Finney	1961	Kevin Keegan	1982
Walter Winterbottom	1963	Bryan Robson	1990
Bobby Moore	1967	Peter Shilton	1991
Bobby Charlton	1969	Brian Clough	1991
Don Revie	1970	Gary Lineker	1992
Gordon Banks	1970	Jimmy Armfield	2000
Jack Charlton	1974	Alan Shearer	2001
Bill Nicholson	1975	Graham Taylor	2002
George Eastham	1975	David Beckham	2003
Joe Mercer	1976	Teddy Sheringham	2007
Emlyn Hughes	1980		

MEMBERS OF THE ORDER OF THE BRITISH EMPIRE (MBE)

Norman Creek	1943	John Barnes	1998
Jimmy Dickinson	1964	Stuart Pearce	1999
Ian Callaghan	1974	Tony Adams	1999
Martin Peters	1978	Viv Anderson	2000
Geoff Hurst	1979	Alan Ball	2000
Trevor Brooking	1981	Steve Bull	2000
Alan Mullery	1975	George Cohen	2000
Terry Paine	1977	Roger Hunt	2000
Tommy Smith	1977	Nobby Stiles	2000
Ray Clemence	1981	Ray Wilson	2000
Mick Mills	1984	Ian Wright	2000
Steve Perryman	1984	Colin Bell	2005
Peter Shilton	1986	Les Ferdinand	2005
Ray Wilkins	1993	Alan Hodgkinson	2008
Gary Mabbutt	1994		

England Managers

Manager	Period
Football Association	30.11.1872 – 24.05.1939
Walter Winterbottom	28.09.1946 – 21.11.1962
Alf Ramsey	27.02.1963 – 03.04.1974
*Joe Mercer	11.05.1974 – 05.06.1974
Don Revie	04.07.1974 – 12.07.1977
Ron Greenwood	07.09.1977 – 05.07.1982
Bobby Robson	22.09.1982 – 07.07.1990
Graham Taylor	12.09.1990 – 17.11.1993
Terry Venables	09.03.1994 – 26.06.1996
Glenn Hoddle	01.09.1996 – 18.11.1998
*Howard Wilkinson	01.02.1999 & 11.10.2000
Kevin Keegan	27.03.1999 – 07.10.2000
*Peter Taylor	15.11.2000
Sven-Goran Eriksson	12.01.2001 – 01.07.2006
Steve McClaren	16.08.2006 – 22.11.2007
Fabio Capello	07.01.2008 – present

* Three of England's 15 managers have been in a caretaker capacity: Joe Mercer had seven games, the three 1974 Home Internationals and a four-match tour of Eastern Europe; Howard Wilkinson took charge the games before and after Kevin Keegan's reign; and Peter Taylor was coach for one match before the arrival of Sven-Goran Eriksson.

DID YOU KNOW THAT?
On 14 December 2007, the Football Association announced that Fabio Capello would take over as England manager from 7 January 2008. Capello's first game was a 2–1 win over Switzerland in a friendly at Wembley on 6 February 2008.

FWA Footballer of the Year

The Football Writers' Association Footballer of the Year has been awarded since 1948 when Stanley Matthews received the honour. There have been 29 English Footballers of the Year, with Matthews, Tom Finney, John Barnes and Gary Lineker winning the award twice. The full list is:

Year	Player	Year	Player
1948	Stanley Matthews	1974	Ian Callaghan
1950	Joe Mercer	1975	Alan Mullery
1951	Harry Johnston	1976	Kevin Keegan
1952	Billy Wright	1977	Emlyn Hughes
1953	Nat Lofthouse	1978	Terry McDermott
1954	Tom Finney	1982	Steve Perryman
1955	Don Revie	1986	Gary Lineker
1957	Tom Finney	1987	Clive Allen
1959	Syd Owen	1988	John Barnes
1960	Bill Slater	1990	John Barnes
1962	Jimmy Adamson	1992	Gary Lineker
1963	Stanley Matthews	1993	Chris Waddle
1964	Bobby Moore	1994	Alan Shearer
1966	Bobby Charlton	2001	Teddy Sheringham
1967	Jack Charlton	2005	Frank Lampard
1969	*Tony Book	2009	Steven Gerrard
1972	Gordon Banks		

* Tony Book shared the award with Scotland's Dave Mackay.

DID YOU KNOW THAT?
Jimmy Adamson and Tony Book are the only two English Footballers of the Year not to win full international honours.

England's Chart Busters

The England World Cup squad have made a number of notable forays into the world of pop music. These are the chartbusters from the aspiring net-busters:

England World Cup Squad

release date	song / label and catalogue number	pos	wks
18 Apr 70 *	**Back Home**		
	Pye 7N 17920	1	16
15 Aug 70	**Back Home** (re-entry)		
	Pye 7N 17920	46	1
10 Apr 82 •	**This Time (We'll Get It Right)/**		
	England We'll Fly the Flag		
	England ER1	2	13
18 Apr 86	**We've Got the Whole World at Our Feet/**		
	When We are Far from Home		
	Columbia DB 9128	66	2
21 May 88	**All the Way***		
	MCA GOAL 1	64	2
2 Jun 90 *	**World in Motion***		
	Factory/MCA FAC 2937	1	12

UK No.1 *   UK Top 10 •

* = England Football Team and the 'sound' of Stock, Aitken and Waterman
** = Englandneworder

Courtesy of *The Book of British Hit Singles & Albums*
by Guinness World Records and the UK Charts Company

DID YOU KNOW THAT?
Paul Gascoigne, Kevin Keegan and Glenn Hoddle and Chris Waddle (the latter pair as a duet) have all released singles.

England's Black Players

Up to the England vs Brazil match in Doha on 14 November 2009, 59 black players had played for England in 135 years of international football, although 107 years elapsed before Viv Anderson made his debut in 1979.

Viv **ANDERSON** · Laurie **CUNNINGHAM** · Cyrille **REGIS**
Ricky **HILL** · Luther **BLISSETT** · Mark **CHAMBERLAIN**
John **BARNES** · Danny **THOMAS** · Brian **STEIN**
Danny **WALLACE** · David **ROCASTLE** · Des **WALKER**
Michael **THOMAS** · Paul **PARKER** · John **FASHANU**
Ian **WRIGHT** · John **SALAKO** · Earl **BARRETT**
Mark **WALTERS** · Brian **DEANE** · Gary **CHARLES**
Andy **GRAY** · Tony **DALEY** · Carlton **PALMER**
Keith **CURLE** · Paul **INCE** · Les **FERDINAND**
Andy **COLE** · Stan **COLLYMORE** · Sol **CAMPBELL**
Ugo **EHIOGU** · David **JAMES** · Rio **FERDINAND**
Dion **DUBLIN** · Wes **BROWN** · Emile **HESKEY**
Kieron **DYER** · Chris **POWELL** · Ashley **COLE**
Trevor **SINCLAIR** · Michael **RICKETTS** · Darius **VASSELL**
Ledley **KING** · Jermaine **JENAS** · Glen **JOHNSON**
Jermain **DEFOE** · Anthony **GARDNER**
Shaun **WRIGHT-PHILLIPS** · Kieran **RICHARDSON**
Zat **KNIGHT** · Darren **BENT** · Theo **WALCOTT**
Aaron **LENNON** · Micah **RICHARDS** · Joleon **LESCOTT**
Ashley **YOUNG** · Gabriel **AGBONLAHOR** · Carlton **COLE**
Tom **HUDDLESTONE**

DID YOU KNOW THAT?
Cyrille Regis was England's first black Under-23 captain. He was born in French Guiana and moved to England aged five.

England's 10 Fastest Goals

17 sec, Tommy Lawton v Portugal — Lisbon, 25 May 1947

27 sec, Bryan Robson v France — Bilbao, 16 June 1982

30 sec, †John Cock v Ireland — Belfast, 25 October 1919

30 sec, †Bill Nicholson v Portugal — Liverpool, 19 May 1951

34 sec, Tommy Lawton v Belgium — Brussels, 21 September 1947

35 sec, Edgar Chadwick v Scotland — Glasgow, 2 April 1892

36 sec, Gareth Southgate v South Africa — Durban, 22 May 2003

38 sec, Bryan Robson v Yugoslavia — Wembley, 13 December 1989

42 sec, Gary Lineker v Malaysia — Kuala Lumpar, 12 June 1991

55 sec, Geoff Hurst v Switzerland — Basle, 13 October 1971

†The goals by Cock and Nicholson were scored on their international debuts.

Busby Babes Remembered

Prior to England's 2–1 friendly win over Switzerland at Wembley Stadium on 6 February 2008 the players from both sides held a minute's silence in tribute to the Manchester United players and others who lost their lives exactly 40 years earlier in the Munich air disaster.

What a Mixture!

The legendary Everton and England centre-forward, Dixie Dean's (16 caps, 18 goals) pre-match meal consisted of a glass of sherry mixed with two raw eggs.

First 10 Countries Beaten by England

Opponent	Score	Date
Scotland (H)	4–2	8 March 1873
Wales (H)	2–1	18 January 1879
Ireland (A)	13–0	18 February 1882
Austria (A)	6–1	6 June 1908
Hungary (A)	11–1	10 June 1908
Bohemia (A)	7–0	13 June 1908
Belgium (A)	2–0	21 May 1921
Northern Ireland (H)	2–0	21 October 1922
France (A)	4–1	10 May 1923
Sweden (A)	4–2	21 May 1923

First 10 Countries to Beat England

Opponent	Score	Date
Scotland (A)	1–2	7 March 1874
Wales (H)	0–1	26 February 1881
Ireland (A)	1–2	15 February 1913
Northern Ireland (A)	1–2	20 October 1923
Spain (A)	3–4	15 May 1929
France (A)	2–5	14 May 1931
Hungary (A)	1–2	10 May 1934
Czechoslovakia (A)	1–2	16 May 1934
Austria (A)	1–2	6 May 1936
Belgium (A)	2–3	9 May 1936

DID YOU KNOW THAT?
England's first Wembley loss came against Scotland in 1928.

England's Golden Oldies

Player	Age
Stanley Matthews	42 years, 104 days
Peter Shilton	40 years, 292 days
Alexander Morten	40 years, 67 days
Frank Osbourne	39 years, 221 days
Edward Taylor	39 years, 40 days
David Seaman	39 years, 27 days
Leslie Compton	38 years, 70 days
Stuart Pearce	37 years, 137 days
Jesse Pennington	36 years, 230 days
Sam Hardy	36 years, 227 days

England's Youngest Debutants

Player	Age
Theo Walcott	17 years, 75 days
Wayne Rooney	17 years, 111 days
James Prinsep	17 years, 252 days
Thurston Rostron	17 years, 311 days
Clement Mitchell	18 years, 23 days
Michael Owen	18 years, 60 days
Micah Richards	18 years, 144 days
Duncan Edwards	18 years, 183 days
James Brown	18 years, 210 days
Arthur Brown	18 years, 328 days

DID YOU KNOW THAT?

Walcott went to the 2006 World Cup finals but didn't play.

First 10 Nations to Draw with England

Opponent	Score	Date
Scotland (A)	0–0	30 November 1872
Wales (H)	1–1	14 March 1885
Ireland (H)	1–1	25 February 1905
Belgium (A)	2–2	1 November 1923
Northern Ireland (A)	0–0	24 October 1925
Germany (A)	3–3	10 May 1930
Austria (A)	0–0	14 May 1930
Italy (A)	1–1	13 May 1933
Denmark (A)	0–0	26 September 1948
Yugoslavia	2–2	22 November 1950

DID YOU KNOW THAT?
The first ever official international, between England and Scotland, ended in a goalless draw. England's next 0–0 draw came on 3 March 1902, against Wales, but it was not until 25 April 1970, at Hampden Park, Glasgow, that an England vs Scotland match didn't see at least one goal.

Theo Gets the Match Ball

When England beat Croatia 4–1 in Zagreb on 10 September 2008 in a FIFA 2010 World Cup qualifying game, Arsenal's Theo Walcott became the youngest player, aged 19 years and 178 days, to score a hat-trick for England, and the first England player to score a hat-trick in a competitive game for England since 21-year-old Michael Owen bagged three against Germany in their 5–1 victory in Munich in 2001.

Literary Lions

In addition to former England players who have published their life stories somewhat prosaically under the title *My Autobiography*, here is a selection of recent autobiographies:

1966 And All That – Sir Geoff Hurst (2001)

Addicted – Tony Adams (1999)

After the Ball – Nobby Stiles (2003)

Being Gazza – Paul Gascoigne (2006)

Butcher: My Autobiography – Terry Butcher (2005)

Carra: My Autobiography – Jamie Carragher (2008)

Farewell but Not Goodbye – Sir Bobby Robson (2005)

Banksy – Gordon Banks (2002)

Biting Talk – Norman Hunter (2004)

Gazza: My Story – Paul Gascoigne (2004)

Greavsie – Jimmy Greaves (2003)

Left Field – Graeme Le Saux (2007)

Mr Wright – Ian Wright (1997)

My Defence – Ashley Cole (2006)

My Side – David Beckham (2003)

My Story – Wayne Rooney (2007)

My World – David Beckham (2001)

Off the Record – Michael Owen (2004)

Playing Extra Time – Alan Ball (2004)

Priceless – Rodney Marsh (2002)

Psycho – Stuart Pearce (2001)

Right Back to the Beginning – Jimmy Armfield (2004)

Safe Hands – David Seaman (2000)

Super Mac – Malcolm Macdonald (2003)

Taking Le Tiss – Matt Le Tissier (2009)

Totally Frank – Frank Lampard Jr (2006)

The Way It Was – Sir Stanley Matthews (2000)

Walking on Water – Brian Clough (2003)

Marching Orders

England players have been shown red cards on only 12 occasions in 881 matches. Ray Wilkins and David Beckham, second time, were captains when they were sent off, while Alan Mullery, Alan Ball, Beckham, first time, and Wayne Rooney, would later captain England.

Alan Mullery v Yugoslavia	Florence on 5 June 1968
Alan Ball v Poland	Chorzow on 6 June 1973
Trevor Cherry v Argentina	Buenos Aires on 12 June 1977
Ray Wilkins v Morocco	Monterrey on 6 June 1986
David Beckham v Argentina	St Etienne on 30 June 30 1998
†**Paul Ince** v Sweden	Stockholm on 5 September 1998
††**Paul Scholes** v Sweden	Wembley on 5 June 1999
David Batty v Poland	Warsaw on 8 September 1999
Alan Smith v Macedonia	Southampton on 16 October 2002
David Beckham v Austria	Old Trafford on 8 October 2005
Wayne Rooney v Portugal	Gelsenkirchen on 1 July 2006
Robert Green v Ukraine	Dnepropetrovsk on 10 October 2009

†This was the first time two England players had been sent off in the same season for England.

††Scholes was the first England player to be sent off on English soil.

DID YOU KNOW THAT?

When Robert Green fouled Artem Milevsky of Ukraine in the 12th minute of England's World Cup qualifier against Ukraine in Dnepropetrovsk on 10 October 2009, he set two unfortunate records. Not only was his dismissal the earliest an England player had been sent off, but he was also the first goalkeeper to see red.

National Football Museum – Players

The National Football Museum is situated at Preston North End's Deepdale Stadium. It was opened on 1 December 2002 with membership open to football figures of any nationality who have made a significant contribution to the English game. The first 29 inductees comprised 22 players, six managers and one woman (Lilly Parr, scorer of over 1,000 goals for Dick Kerr's Ladies team, the unofficial women's world champions in the 1920s and 1930s), and were selected from a shortlist of 96 nominees by a panel of 20 football experts.

The players inducted in 2009 took to 46 the number of present or former England internationals in the Hall of Fame.

Player	Inducted	Player	Inducted
Cliff Bastin	2009	Viv Anderson	2004
Trevor Brooking	2009	Geoff Hurst	2004
George Cohen	2009	Wilf Mannion	2004
Len Shackleton	2009	Alan Shearer	2004
Teddy Sheringham	2009	Alan Ball	2003
Frank Swift	2009	Tommy Lawton	2003
Jimmy Armfield	2008	Gary Lineker	2003
David Beckham	2008	Stan Mortensen	2003
Steve Bloomer	2008	Gordon Banks	2002
Emlyn Hughes	2008	Bobby Charlton	2002
Paul Scholes	2008	Dixie Dean	2002
Ray Wilson	2008	Duncan Edwards	2002
Peter Beardsley	2007	Tom Finney	2002
Glenn Hoddle	2007	Paul Gascoigne	2002
Nobby Stiles	2007	Jimmy Greaves	2002
Roger Hunt	2006	Johnny Haynes	2002
Jackie Milburn	2006	Kevin Keegan	2002
Martin Peters	2006	Nat Lofthouse	2002
John Barnes	2005	Stanley Matthews	2002
Colin Bell	2005	Bobby Moore	2002
Jack Charlton	2005	Bryan Robson	2002
Ian Wright	2005	Peter Shilton	2002
Tony Adams	2004	Billy Wright	2002

Nicknames of England Players

Beats	James Beattie
Big Al	Alan Shearer
Bite Yer Legs	Norman Hunter
Bogota Bandit	Charlie Mitten
Butch	Ray Wilkins
Crazy Horse	Emlyn Hughes
Fatty	William Foulke
Gazza	Paul Gascoigne
Golden Balls	David Beckham
Happy	Nobby Stiles
Lamps	Frank Lampard (Jr)
Lion of Vienna	Nat Lofthouse
Merlin	Gordon Hill
Mooro	Bobby Moore
Morty	Stan Mortensen
Nijinsky	Colin Bell
Pancho	Stuart Pearson
Pongo	Thomas Waring
Psycho	Stuart Pearce
Roonaldo	Wayne Rooney
Shaggy	Steve McManaman
Sicknote	Darren Anderton
Super Kev	Kevin Keegan
The Cat	Bert Williams & Peter Bonetti
The Giraffe	Jackie Charlton
Wizard of the Dribble	Stanley Matthews
Wor Jackie	Jackie Milburn

DID YOU KNOW THAT?
The England team has no official nickname.

No Place Like Home

Wembley Stadium did not become England's "official home" until January 1966. Here is a list of all of England's home grounds:

ALEXANDRA MEADOWS, Blackburn • *ANFIELD,* Liverpool
ASHTON GATE, Bristol City • *AYRESOME PARK,* Middlesbrough
THE BASEBALL GROUND, Derby • *BLOOMFIELD ROAD,* Blackpool
BRAMALL LANE, Sheffield • *THE CITY GROUND,* Nottingham
CITY OF MANCHESTER STADIUM, Manchester
COUNTY GROUND, Derby • *CRAVEN COTTAGE,* London
THE CRYSTAL PALACE, London • *THE DELL,* Southampton
THE DEN, London • *ELLAND ROAD,* Leeds
EWOOD PARK, Blackburn • *FRATTON PARK,* Portsmouth
GOODISON PARK, Liverpool • *THE HAWTHORNS,* West Bromwich
HIGHBURY, London • *HILLSBOROUGH,* Sheffield
KENNINGTON OVAL, London • *LEAMINGTON ROAD,* Blackburn
LEEDS ROAD, Huddersfield • *LIVERPOOL CRICKET CLUB,* Aigburth
MAINE ROAD, Manchester • *MOLINEUX,* Wolverhampton
NEWCASTLE ROAD, Sunderland • *NANTWICH ROAD,* Crewe
OLD TRAFFORD, Manchester • *PARK AVENUE,* Bradford
PERRY BARR, Birmingham • *PORTMAN ROAD,* Ipswich
PRIDE PARK, Derby • *QUEEN'S CLUB,* London
RICHMOND ATHLETIC GROUND, London • *RIVERSIDE,* Middlesbrough
ROKER PARK, Sunderland • *ST JAMES'S PARK,* Newcastle
ST MARY'S, Southampton • *SELHURST PARK,* London
STADIUM OF LIGHT, Sunderland • *STAMFORD BRIDGE,* London
TRENT BRIDGE, Nottingham • *TURF MOOR,* Burnley
UPTON PARK, London • *VICTORIA GROUND,* Stoke
VILLA PARK, Birmingham • *THE WALKERS STADIUM,* Leicester
WHALLEY RANGE, Manchester • *WHITE HART LANE,* London

On the Spot

A total of 27 goalkeepers have faced a penalty kick (not in a shoot-out) while playing for England:

Goalkeeper	Career	Clubs Played For	Faced	Saved/ Missed
John Robinson	1897–1901	Derby Co, New Brighton Tower, Southampton	1	1 (M)
William Rowley	1889–1902	Stoke City	1	1 (M)
John Hillman	1899	Burnley	1	None
William George	1902	Aston Villa	1	1 (S)
Sam Hardy	1907–1920	Liverpool, Aston Villa	3	1 (S)
Horace Bailey	1908	Leicester Fosse	1	1 (M)
Arthur Hufton	1923–1929	West Ham United	1	None
John Brown	1927–1929	Sheffield Wednesday	1	None
Benjamin Olney	1928	Aston Villa	1	None
Henry Hibbs	1929–1936	Birmingham	3	3 (1S/2M)
Ted Sagar	1935–1936	Everton	1	None
Frank Swift	1946–1949	Manchester City	1	None
Ted Ditchburn	1948–1956	Tottenham Hotspur	1	None
Bert Williams	1949–1955	Wolverhampton Wanderers	2	None
Gil Merrick	1951–1954	Birmingham City	3	None
Eddie Hopkinson	1957–1959	Bolton Wanderers	1	None
Ron Springett	1959–1966	Sheffield Wednesday	3	2 (S)
Gordon Banks	1963–1972	Leicester City, Stoke City	5	1 (S)
Peter Shilton	1970–1990	Leicester C, Stoke C, Nottingham F, Derby Co, Southampton	15	2 (1S/1M)
Ray Clemence	1972–1983	Liverpool, Tottenham Hotspur	8	1 (S)
Chris Woods	1985–1993	Norwich City, Glasgow Rangers, Sheffield Wed	1	None
David Seaman	1988–2002	QPR, Arsenal	3	1 (S)
Nigel Martyn	1992–2002	Crystal Palace, Leeds Utd	3	1 (S)
David James	1997–pres	Liverpool, Aston Villa, West Ham, Manchester C, Portsmouth	6	2 (M)
Richard Wright	2000–2001	Ipswich Town, Arsenal	2	1 (S)
Paul Robinson	2003–pres	Leeds Utd, Tottenham Hotspur Blackburn Rovers	2	1 (S)
Ben Foster	2007–pres	Manchester United	1	1 (M)

Scoring at the Wrong End

The following England players have scored own goals since 1945:

Gary Neville v Croatia	11 October 2006
Richard Wright v Malta	3 June 2000
Tony Adams v Holland	23 March 1988
Phil Neal v Australia	19 June 1983
Phil Thompson v Wales	17 May 1980
Colin Todd v Scotland	18 May 1974
Jimmy Dickinson v Belgium	17 June 1954
Leslie Compton v Yugoslavia	22 November 1950

DID YOU KNOW THAT?
Richard Wright conceded and saved a penalty against Malta.

National Football Museum – Managers

Seven former England managers have been inducted into the Hall of Fame at the National Football Museum:

Manager	Inducted
Joe Mercer	2009
Terry Venables	2007
Ron Greenwood	2006
Walter Winterbottom	2005
Don Revie	2004
Bobby Robson	2003
Alf Ramsey	2002

Penalty Shoot-Out Fallguys

And the fallguys are: **1990 World Cup** – Stuart Pearce and Chris Waddle against Germany; **Euro 96** – Gareth Southgate against Germany; **1998 King Hassan II Cup** – Rob Lee and Les Ferdinand against Belgium; **1998 World Cup** – Paul Ince and David Batty against Argentina; **Euro 2004** – David Beckham and Darius Vassell against Portugal. **2006 World Cup** – Jamie Carragher, Steven Gerrard and Frank Lampard against Portugal.

England lost all six of these penalty shoot-outs. The only time they won a penalty shoot-out was in their Euro 96 quarter-final encounter with Spain at Wembley. The score was 4–2. (Spain missed two penalties, so England did not need to take a fifth one.)

DID YOU KNOW THAT?
When Jamie Carragher missed against Portugal, it was his second attempt. He scored with his first try, but the referee ordered a retake because he hadn't blown his whistle.

South Africa Bound

When England beat Croatia 5–1 at Wembley on 9 September 2009, it secured England's qualification for the 2010 FIFA World Cup finals in South Africa. It was the first time that England had qualified for a World Cup Finals by winning at Wembley since Bobby Robson's team qualified for the 1986 finals. It was also the first time England had secured World Cup qualification with two games to spare in their group.

PFA Players' Player of the Year

The Professional Football Association's Players' Player of the Year was introduced in 1974. The award goes to the player who, in the opinion of his fellow professionals, was the outstanding English League player of the season. Since its inception, 16 England internationals have won the award 17 times, with Alan Shearer winning it twice.

Year	Player	Club
1974	Norman Hunter	Leeds Utd
1975	Colin Todd	Derby County
1978	Peter Shilton	Nottingham Forest
1980	Terry McDermott	Liverpool
1982	Kevin Keegan	Southampton
1985	Peter Reid	Everton
1986	Gary Lineker	Everton
1987	Clive Allen	Tottenham Hotspur
1988	John Barnes	Liverpool
1990	David Platt	Aston Villa
1992	Gary Pallister	Manchester United
1995	Alan Shearer	Blackburn Rovers
1996	Les Ferdinand	Newcastle United
1997	Alan Shearer	Newcastle United
2001	Teddy Sheringham	Manchester United
2005	John Terry	Chelsea
2006	Steven Gerrard	Liverpool

DID YOU KNOW THAT?

Norman Hunter's mistake led to the goal which saw Poland deny England a place in the 1974 World Cup finals, but his fellow professionals still voted him their Player of the Year.

Record England Appearances

Player	Clubs/Career	Caps	Gls
Peter Shilton	Leicester City, Stoke City, Nottingham Forest, Southampton, Derby County, 1971–90	**125**	0
David Beckham	Man Utd, Real Madrid, LA Galaxy Milan, 1996–present	**115**	17
Bobby Moore	West Ham Utd, 1962–74	**108**	2
Bobby Charlton	Man Utd, 1958–70	**106**	49
Billy Wright	Wolves, 1947–59	**105**	3
Bryan Robson	WBA, Man Utd, 1980–92	**90**	26
Michael Owen	Liverpool, Real Madrid, Newcastle, Man Utd, 1998–present	**89**	40
Kenny Sansom	Crystal Palace, Arsenal, 1979–88	**86**	1
Gary Neville	Man Utd, 1995–present	**87**	0
Ray Wilkins	Chelsea, Man Utd, Milan, 1976–87	**84**	3
Gary Lineker	Leicester City, Everton, Barcelona, Spurs, 1984–92	**80**	48
John Barnes	Watford, Liverpool, 1983–95	**79**	11
Stuart Pearce	Nottingham Forest, West Ham Utd, 1987–99	**78**	4
Terry Butcher	Ipswich T, Rangers, 1980–90	**77**	3
Steven Gerrard	Liverpool, 2000–present	**77**	16
Ashley Cole	Arsenal, Chelsea, 2001–present	**77**	2
Tom Finney	Preston North End, 1947–59	**76**	30
Rio Ferdinand	West Ham, Leeds Utd, Man Utd, 1997–present	**76**	3
Frank Lampard	West Ham Utd, Chelsea, 1999–present	**76**	20
David Seaman	Queens Park Rangers, Arsenal, 1988–2002	**75**	0

DID YOU KNOW THAT?

When Michael Owen scored England's second goal in their 3–2 defeat against Romania in Toulouse in 1998, he became the country's youngest ever goalscorer in the World Cup finals at 18 years and 194 days.

Record Attendances

Home

100,000 England v Austria   *WEMBLEY*, 28 November 1951
100,000 England v Hungary   *WEMBLEY*, 23 November 1953
100,000 England v West Germany   *WEMBLEY*, 1 December 1954
100,000 England v USSR   *WEMBLEY*, 22 October 1958
100,000 England v Portugal   *WEMBLEY*, 25 October 1961
100,000 England v Rest of World   *WEMBLEY*, 23 October 1963
100,000 England v Spain   *WEMBLEY*, 3 April 1968
100,000 England v Portugal   *WEMBLEY*, 10 December 1969
100,000 England v Northern Ireland   *WEMBLEY*, 21 April 1970
100,000 England v West Germany   *WEMBLEY*, 29 April 1972
100,000 England v Poland   *WEMBLEY*, 17 October 1973
100,000 England v West Germany   *WEMBLEY*, 12 March 1975
100,000 England v Scotland   *WEMBLEY*, 26 May 1979

Away

160,000 Brazil v England   *MARACANA*, Rio, 13 May 1959
149,547 England v Scotland   *HAMPDEN* Park, 17 April 1937

Absent Friend

Sven-Goran Eriksson is the only permanent England coach never to have led an England team out at either the old or the new Wembley Stadium. Kevin Keegan was in charge of England when they played their last match at the old Wembley on 7 October 2000. The first match at the new stadium was on 1 June 2007, by which time Steve McClaren was the England manager.

Top 10 Goalies

England's 10 most capped goalkeepers are:

	Caps
Peter Shilton	125
David Seaman	75
Gordon Banks	73
Ray Clemence	61
David James	48
Chris Woods	43
Paul Robinson	41
Ron Springett	33
Harry Hibbs	25
Bert Williams	24

DID YOU KNOW THAT?
Neither Ray Clemence nor David James has ever appeared in a World Cup finals match, but both have been on the bench. Clemence was in the 1982 squad and was England's goalkeeping coach in 1998, 2002 and 2006, while James was in the squads for both the 2002 and 2006 tournaments.

Fab's Four

When England played Trinidad & Tobago in a friendly at Port-of-Spain, Trinidad on 1 June 2008, coach Fabio Capello gave four players their first full England caps: striker Dean Ashton (West Ham United), goalkeeper Joe Hart (Manchester City) and defenders Phil Jagielka (Everton) and Stephen Warnock (Blackburn Rovers). England won 3–0.

Top England Goalscorers

Player	Teams	Goals	Games
Bobby Charlton	Man Utd, 1958–70	49	106
Gary Lineker	Leicester City, Everton, Barcelona, Spurs, 1984–92	48	80
Jimmy Greaves	Chelsea, Spurs, 1959–67	44	57
Michael Owen	Liverpool, Real Madrid, Newcastle Utd, Man Utd, 1998–present	40	89
Nat Lofthouse	Bolton Wanderers, 1951–59	30	33
Alan Shearer	Southampton, Blackburn Rovers, Newcastle Utd, 1992–2000	30	63
Tom Finney	Preston North End, 1947–59	30	76
Vivian Woodward	Spurs, Chelsea, 1903–11	29	23
Steve Bloomer	Derby County, Middlesbrough, 1895–1907	28	23
David Platt	Aston Villa, Bari, Juventus, Sampdoria, Arsenal, 1990–96	27	62
Bryan Robson	WBA, Man Utd, 1980–92	26	90
Wayne Rooney	Everton, Manchester Utd, 2003–present	25	57
Geoff Hurst	West Ham, 1966–72	24	49
Stan Mortensen	Blackpool, 1947–54	23	25
Tommy Lawton	Everton, Chelsea, Notts Co, 1939–49	22	23
Mick Channon	Southampton, Man City, 1972–77	21	46
Kevin Keegan	Liverpool, SV Hamburg, Southampton, 1972–82	21	63
Martin Peters	West Ham Utd, Tottenham, 1966–74	20	67
Frank Lampard	West Ham Utd, Chelsea, 1999–present	20	76

DID YOU KNOW THAT?

Five players are tied for 20th place with 18 goals: Dixie Dean, George Camsell, Johnny Haynes, Roger Hunt and Peter Crouch. David Beckham is just one goal behind these five.

Unbeaten Streaks

England's longest unbeaten streak stands at 20 matches played between the 3–2 home loss to Scotland on 13 April 1889 and the 2–1 away loss to Scotland on 4 April 1896. England's record during this seven-year streak was 16 wins and four draws. In the nineteenth century England played only three times per year, once each against the other home countries, Scotland, Wales and Ireland, in the British Championship. Of those 20 matches, nine were played at home.

The second longest unbeaten streak, and the longest since World War II, involved the 19 matches played between the 3–2 home loss to Austria in a friendly on 20 October 1965 and the 3–2 Home International Championship loss to Scotland on 15 April 1967. England's record during this 18-month streak, which also included winning the World Cup, was 16 wins and three draws. Of the 19 matches, 12 were at home.

The third longest unbeaten streak stands at 18 matches played between the 2–1 away loss to Scotland on 7 April 1906 and the 2–0 away loss to Scotland on 2 April 1910. England's record during this streak, which included their first ever games against continental European opposition (in 1908 and 1909), was 14 wins and four draws. Of these 18 matches, seven were at home.

England also had a 17-match unbeaten streak between the 3–1 loss to the USSR at the 1988 European Championship finals in West Germany on 18 June 1988 and the 2–1 loss to Uruguay in a friendly at Wembley on 22 May 1990. England's record during this 23-month streak was 10 wins and seven draws. Of the 17 games played, 10 were at home.

The Wally with the Brolly

England went into the final group game of their Euro 2008 qualifying campaign, against Croatia at Wembley on 21 November 2007, knowing a draw would be good enough to secure their place at the finals in Austria and Switzerland. Their hopes of qualifying had been dented when Russia beat them 2–1 in Moscow a month earlier, but Israel threw England a lifeline by beating the Russians 2–1 in Tel Aviv on 17 November, confirming Croatia's qualification. However, on a rainy night and a difficult pitch, England fell behind 2–0, fought back to make it 2–2, only to concede a late winner to the Croats. The following day the England manager, Steve McClaren – who had watched the game standing rather ingloriously underneath a large red and blue umbrella – paid the price of failure and was sacked by the FA. Rumours linked Jose Mourinho, among others, with the vacant position before Fabio Capello was announced as the England coach in December 2007.

DID YOU KNOW THAT?
Steve McClaren followed in the footsteps of another former England coach by managing a Dutch club. Bobby Robson was hired by PSV Eindhoven in 1990, while AZ Alkmaar took on McClaren in the summer of 2008.

England Get Lucky in 2010 Draw

England were among the top seeds and placed in Group C for the 2010 World Cup with Slovenia, Algeria and the USA.

World Cup Finals Record

Year	Rank	Teams	Stage Reached	P	W	D	L	F	A	GD	Pts
1930	-	-	Did not enter	-	-	-	-	-	-	-	-
1934	-	-	Did not enter	-	-	-	-	-	-	-	-
1938	-	-	Did not enter	-	-	-	-	-	-	-	-
1950	8	13	1st phase group	3	1	0	2	2	2	0	2
1954	7	16	Quarter-finals	3	1	1	1	8	8	0	3
1958	10	16	1st phase group play-off	4	0	3	1	4	5	−1	3
1962	8	16	Quarter-finals	4	1	1	2	5	6	−1	3
1966	1	16	Final	6	5	1	0	11	3	+8	11
1970	8	16	Quarter-finals	4	2	0	2	4	4	0	4
1974	-	-	Failed to qualify	-	-	-	-	-	-	-	-
1978	-	-	Failed to qualify	-	-	-	-	-	-	-	-
1982	6	24	2nd phase group	5	3	2	0	6	1	+5	8
1986	8	24	Quarter-finals	5	2	1	2	7	3	+4	5
1990	4	24	Semi-final / fourth place	7	3	3	1	8	6	+2	9
1994	-	-	Failed to qualify	-	-	-	-	-	-	-	-
1998	9	32	Round of 16 teams	4	2	1	1	7	4	+3	7
2002	6	32	Quarter-finals	5	2	2	1	6	3	+3	8
2006	-	32	Quarter-finals	5	3	1	1	6	2	+4	10

DID YOU KNOW THAT?

England went 1–0 down when they went out 2–1 to Argentina in 1986, to Germany on penalties in 1990, to Argentina, again, in 1998, also on penalties. However, when Brazil beat England 2–1 in 2002, it was England who had taken the lead. In 2006, the match with Portugal ended goalless before penalty shoot-out heart-break struck again.

World Cup Hat-Trick Heroes

Two England players have scored a hat-trick in the World Cup finals. Geoff Hurst is the only player from any country to score a hat-trick in the World Cup Final, which he did in England's 4–2 extra-time victory over West Germany on 30 July 1966 at Wembley. Gary Lineker became the only England player to score a hat-trick in the first 90 minutes in a World Cup finals game, when he scored all three goals in England's 3–0 win against Poland on 11 June 1986.

DID YOU KNOW THAT?
In the 21st century, Michael Owen and Theo Walcott scored hat-tricks in World Cup qualifiers, both away from home, against Germany in 2001 and Croatia in 2008, respectively.

Beckham's Armband Four-Timer

David Beckham has won the captain's armband under four different England managers: Peter Taylor, Sven-Goran Eriksson, Steve McClaren and Fabio Capello.

Not Always an England Hero

Fabio Capello won 32 caps as a midfielder for Italy. On 14 June 1973 he scored against England in a 2–0 win at Stadio Comunale, Turin and on 14 November that same year, Capello scored the winner against England at Wembley.

Zieg Heil Indignity

This match is remembered more for the England players giving the Nazi salute during the pre-game ceremony in Berlin's packed Olympic Stadium on 14 May 1938, than it is for the 6–3 thumping England gave the Nazi regime's sporting pride and joy that day. The game was Germany's last match before the 1938 World Cup finals in France, and after a 16-match unbeaten run, which included 10 straight victories, the Germans were full of confidence.

Prior to the kick-off, at the direction of the British Ambassador to Germany, Sir Neville Henderson, who was supported by Stanley Rous, the Secretary of the FA, the England players joined in the raised arm fascist salute as the German national anthem was being played, while leading members of the Nazi party Goering, Goebbels, Hess and von Ribbentrop watched.

Only captain Eddie Hapgood and Cliff Bastin had made more than ten international appearances for England prior to the game. Indeed England's left-half, Don Welsh, and centre-forward, Frank Broome, were making their debuts while the inside-right, Jackie Robinson, was winning only his second cap. The England team that day in Berlin was:

England: Woodley, Sproston, Hapgood, Willingham, Young, Welsh, Matthews, Robinson, Broome, Goulden, Bastin.

DID YOU KNOW THAT?
England did not play any official internationals between 24 May 1939 and 28 September 1946, and of the England team that played in Berlin on 14 May 1938, only Stanley Matthews played international football after the end of World War II.

Old Foes and New for Euro 2012

When the draw for the qualifying rounds of Euro 2012 was made in Warsaw, Poland, on 7 February 2010, England were one of the top seeds. In Group G England will face Switzerland, Bulgaria, Wales and Montenegro. England have played Wales on 100 occasions since 1879 winning 64 times and losing 15, but have never met Montenegro since they became an independent state. In eight games against Bulgaria, England have four wins and four draws, while they have won 13 and drawn four of 20 matches against Swtizerland. The 2012 finals will be co-hosted by Poland and Ukraine.

Rio Gets the Armband

Rio Ferdinand was appointed England captain after former skipper John Terry was stripped of the honour on 5 February 2010.

World Cup Players and Managers

Three men have played for England in World Cup finals and later managed the squad in finals tournaments too: Sir Alf Ramsey played in 1950 and managed in 1966 and 1970; Sir Bobby Robson played in 1958 and was coach in 1986 and 1990; and Glenn Hoddle appeared in 1982 and 1986 and was in charge of the team in 1998.

First and Last

Everyone knows of England's famous third goal of the 1966 World Cup Final, the one awarded by the Russian – from Azerbaijan actually – linesman Tofik Bakhramov. What few know is that he also ran the line in England's opening game, the 0–0 draw with Uruguay, or that the Azeri national stadium in Baku is named in his honour.

Coles like London Buses

No player with the surname Cole played for England for 122 years until, on 29 March 1995, Andy Cole made his debut as a substitute against Uruguay at Wembley. Since then, rather like London buses, there have been a lot of them, and four different Coles have earned a combined 151 caps: Andy won 15, Ashley has 77, Carlton has six and Joe has 53. Amazingly none of the four are related in any way, though, Ashley, Carlton and Joe have played for Chelsea, and Andy is the only one to play for England when not with a London club.

Two Villans Grab Nine Goals

England's first ever match against Ireland, on 18 February 1892, ended with a 13–0 victory in Belfast. Two Aston Villa players, Howard Vaughton, five, and Arthur Brown, four, scored nine of the goals.

CHAPTER

6

FOR CLUB
AND COUNTRY

This section is a great one for settling arguments about the England team, the players and their clubs. England have played more than 880 international matches since the first ever game in November 1872 and more than 1,160 players have appeared in at least one international.

No less than 36 current Premier League or Football League clubs (plus Luton Town, Cambridge University, Corinthians, Oxford University and the Wanderers) have supplied at least ten men who have appeared in an England international while at those clubs. And, in most cases, their 10 most recent internationals have been capped in the last 60 or so years. There isn't space here for all 41 clubs, but here are a couple of dozen to keep you amused.

Aston Villa lead the way in providing the most England internationals with 68, but Manchester United's players have earned the most caps, more than 1,000, and scored the most goals, approaching 200. For some clubs, such as Villa and United, all the players are of recent vintage and they are all household names. Then again, when you look at West Bromwich Albion, Charlton Athletic and other clubs no longer playing in the top division, you might be left thinking, "who was he?" "why did they pick him?" or "where did he play?"

England's Last 10 Addicks

Player	Years
George Armitage	1925
Harold Hobbis	1936
Don Welsh	1938–39
Derek Ufton	1953
Mike Bailey	1964–65
Chris Powell	2001–02
Paul Konchesky	2003
Scott Parker	2003
Luke Young	2005
Darren Bent	2006

DID YOU KNOW THAT?

England have never fielded two Charlton Athletic players at the same time in a game. However, Scott Parker was an unused substitute when Paul Konchesky won his only England cap in their 3–1 defeat to Australia at Upton Park on 12 February 2003. England used 11 substitutes in that match. A total of 12 Charlton Athletic players have been capped by England.

DID YOU KNOW THAT?

In the 1940s and 50s, Charlton Athletic's stadium, the Valley, boasted one of the largest capacities in British football. It could hold more than 70,000 fans, and although average attendances of more than 40,000 were commonplace, the ground was rarely, if ever, completely full. It is built, as the name says, in a valley and part of the old terracing is still visible in the renovated ground, which has a capacity of just over 27,000.

England's Last 10 Baggies

Player	Years
Bobby Robson	1957–62
Jeff Astle	1969–70
Tony Brown	1971
Peter Barnes	1979–81
Laurie Cunningham	1979
Bryan Robson	1980–81
Cyrille Regis	1981–82
Derek Statham	1983
Steve Hunt	1984
Scott Carson	2008

DID YOU KNOW THAT?

The former England manager, Bobby Robson, the former England trainer, Don Howe, and Derek Kevan, all from WBA, started together in the same England line-up on four occasions. They played against the USSR on 18 May 1958, and in three World Cup finals matches against the USSR, Brazil and Austria in June 1958. A total of 42 West Brom players have been capped by England.

DID YOU KNOW THAT?

The Hawthorns, the home of West Bromwich Albion, has staged two full England internationals; on 21 October 1922, England defeated Northern Ireland 2–0 and on 8 December 1924 Belgium were beaten 4–0. The stadium is also the highest above sea level of any ground in the Football Leaue and Premier League. It is 551 feet (168 metres) above sea level. In 2000 and 2001, the Hawthorns hosted the popular Indian sport of Kabbadi.

England's Last 10 Black Cats

Player	Years
Len Shackleton	1948–54
Willie Watson	1949–50
Colin Grainger	1957
Stan Anderson	1962
Dave Watson	1974–75
Tony Towers	1976
Nick Pickering	1983
Kevin Phillips	1999–2002
Michael Gray	1999
Gavin McCann	2001

DID YOU KNOW THAT?
Three Sunderland players started for England against Ireland in Belfast on 15 February 1913: Charlie Buchan, Francis Cuggy and John Mordue. Buchan scored for England in a 2–1 defeat. A total of 24 Sunderland players have been capped by England.

DID YOU KNOW THAT?
Both Sunderland's present home, the Stadium of Light, and its former home, Roker Park, have staged full England international matches. Famous architect Archibald Leitch was responsible for Roker Park, which was also used during the 1966 World Cup for three group matches and the quarter-final between the Soviet Union and Hungary, won 2–1 by the USSR. The Stadium of Light opened in 1997. Two years later, on 10 October 1999, England defeated Belgium 2–1 in a friendly at the Stadium of Light and on 2 April 2003, Turkey were beaten 2–0 in a European Championship qualifier.

England's Last 10 Boro Boys

Player	Years
Gary Pallister	1988–89
Nicky Barmby	1995–96
Paul Gascoigne	1997–98
Paul Merson	1998
Paul Ince	1999–2000
Ugo Ehiogu	2001–02
Gareth Southgate	2001–04
Danny Mills (on loan from Leeds United)	2004
Stewart Downing	2005–09
Jonathan Woodgate	2007–08

DID YOU KNOW THAT?

Brian Clough and Ed Holliday played together twice in the same England team. They both made their England debuts against Wales on 17 October 1959 in a 1–1 draw in Cardiff (Jimmy Greaves scored for England). They also started together 11 days later against Sweden in a 3–2 defeat at Wembley on 28 October 1959. A total of 29 Middlesbrough players have been capped by England.

DID YOU KNOW THAT?

Middlesbrough's Riverside Stadium was the first one in England to be built to comply with the Taylor Report following the 1989 Hillsborough Disaster. It opened in August 1995, replacing Ayresome Park as Boro's home. In the only full international to be played at the Riverside, a 2–1 Engand victory against Slovakia on 11 June 2003, there were Boro players on both sides. Gareth Southgate of England marked Slovakian striker Szilard Nemeth.

England's Last 10 Brummie Blues

Player	Years
Lewis Stoker	1932–34
Arthur Grosvenor	1933
Gil Merrick	1951–54
Jeffrey Hall	1955–57
Gordon Astall	1956
Trevor Smith	1959
Mike Hellawell	1962
Trevor Francis	1977–78
Matthew Upson	2003–04
Emile Heskey	2004

DID YOU KNOW THAT?

Two Birmingham City players started for England for the first time on 5 April 1930 when goalkeeper Harry Hibbs and Joe Bradford played against Scotland. A total of 16 Birmingham City players have been capped by England up to the end of 2005.

DID YOU KNOW THAT?

In October 2009 Birmingham City became yet another of the growing number of British clubs to fall under overseas ownership when Carson Yeung, a Hong Kong-based businessman, bought out the interests of David Gold and David Sullivan. For many years, the Blues had been almost unique in British football in that the club's managing director was a woman, Karren Brady. Ms Brady married a former Blues player, Canadian international Paul Peschisolido in 1995, who had been transferred away from St Andrews a year earlier.

England's Last 10 City Blues

Player	Years
David White	1992
Trevor Sinclair	2003
David James	2004–06
Shaun Wright-Phillips	2004–05, 2009–present
Micah Richards	2006–present
Joey Barton	2007
Joe Hart	2008–present
Wayne Bridge	2009–present
Gareth Barry	2009–present
Joleon Lescott	2009–present

DID YOU KNOW THAT?
When England played Brazil in an international friendly at the Khalifi International Stadium, Doha, Qatar on 14 November 2009, four Manchester City players started an international for England for the first time: Gareth Barry, Wayne Bridge, Joleon Lescott and Shaun Wright-Phillips.

DID YOU KNOW THAT?
The first Manchester City player to manage England was Don Revie, who had played for England in the 1950s and succeeded Sir Alf Ramsey in 1974. However, no fewer than three other England managers have been City manager before or after becoming national coach. Joe Mercer, who was caretaker manager between Ramsey and Revie, led City to great success in the late 1960s and early 70s. Kevin Keegan spent four years in charge at City after he had stepped down as England manager and Sven-Goran Eriksson was manager at Eastlands for the 2007–08 season.

England's Last 10 Clarets

Player	Years
Billy Elliott	1952
Brian Pilkington	1954
Colin McDonald	1958
John Connelly	1959–63
John Angus	1961
George Miller	1961
Ray Pointer	1961
Gordon Harris	1966
Ralph Coates	1970
Martin Dobson	1974

DID YOU KNOW THAT?

Two Burnley players have started at the same time for England on 10 different occasions between 1922 and 1961. The last pairing was Ray Pointer and John Connelly, who played in England's 2–0 win over Portugal at Wembley on 25 October 1961, and both players scored. A total of 24 Burnley players have been capped by England.

DID YOU KNOW THAT?

Burnley's home has been Turf Moor since before the advent of the Football League. The stadium opened in 1883, some five years before Burnley became one the League's 12 founder members. In 1987 Burnley almost became the first post-war League Champions to lose their Football League status. The 1960 League Champions went into the last match of the season needing a victory to retain their place in the Fourth Division. A 2–1 victory over Leyton Orient and a defeat for Lincoln saw the Imps go down.

England's Last 10 Cottagers

Player	Years
Leonard Oliver	1929
Albert Barrett	1929
John Arnold	1933
James Taylor	1951
Bedford Jezzard	1954–55
Johnny Haynes	1954–62
Jim Langley	1958
George Cohen	1964–67
Zat Knight	2005–07
Bobby Zamora	2009–present

DID YOU KNOW THAT?

On only four occasions have two Fulham players appeared in the same England team. This most recently occurred when Jim Langley and Johnny Haynes played together in the 5–0 defeat to Yugoslavia in Belgrade on 11 May 1958.

DID YOU KNOW THAT?

The only Fulham player to win more than 50 full England caps was midfielder Johnny Haynes, who played for the Cottagers from 1952 to 1970 and for England 1954–62. Haynes was nicknamed "The Maestro" but his illustrious international career (he had captained England 22 times), was effectively ended by a 1962 car crash. Fulham did have one member of the 1966 World Cup-winning squad, right-back George Cohen, another loyal one-club man. The Cohen family was involved in another famous England World Cup success when George's nephew, Ben, played in the 2003 Rugby Union team which lifted the Webb Ellis trophy.

England's Last 10 Eagles

Player	Years
John Alderson	1923
John Byrne	1961
Peter Taylor	1976
Kenny Sansom	1979–80
Ian Wright	1991
Geoff Thomas	1991–92
John Salako	1991
Andy Gray	1991
Nigel Martyn	1992–93
Andy Johnson	2005

DID YOU KNOW THAT?

Three Crystal Palace players started for England when they beat New Zealand 2–0 in Auckland in 1991 – Geoff Thomas, Ian Wright and John Salako – while Nigel Martyn was an unused substitute. A total of 11 Crystal Palace players have been capped by England.

DID YOU KNOW THAT?

Terry Venables became manager of Crystal Palace in 1976 and quickly developed a fine reputation as a coach. The former midfielder, who won two full caps as a player, later became England coach and was in charge of the team when they hosted Euro 96, losing on penalties to Germany. Another Palace player to be in charge of the national team was Peter Taylor, who made his reputation as coach of the England Under-21s team. After Kevin Keegan quit as coach, Taylor managed England in the friendly defeat against Italy on 15 November 2000, before returning to Under-21s duty.

England's Last 10 Forest Reds

Player	Years
Peter Davenport	1985
Stuart Pearce	1987–97
Neil Webb	1987–89
Steve Hodge	1988–91
Des Walker	1988–92
Nigel Clough	1989–93
Gary Charles	1991
Stan Collymore	1995
Colin Cooper	1995
Steve Stone	1995–96

DID YOU KNOW THAT?
Four Nottingham Forest players were in the starting line-up for England against Sweden on 10 June 1979. Viv Anderson, Trevor Francis, Peter Shilton and Tony Woodcock were part of Forest's 1979 European Cup-winning team that played in England's 0–0 draw in Stockholm that day. A total of 37 Nottingham Forest players have been capped by England.

DID YOU KNOW THAT?
Although no Nottingham Forest player or manager has been England coach, Stuart Pearce was coach of the Under-21s squad for many years and was promoted to be an assistant to Fabio Capello at the same time as running the Under-21s. The one Forest boss who should have had England's top job was Brian Clough, the man who took Forest out of Division Two and won a League Championship and two European Cups. Forest remain the only club in Europe with more European Cup successes than domestic League titles.

England's Last 10 Foxes

Player	Years
Septimus Smith	1935
Gordon Banks	1963–67
Peter Shilton	1970–75
Keith Weller	1974
Frank Worthington	1974
Steve Whitworth	1975
Gary Lineker	1984–85
Emile Heskey	1999–2000
Steve Guppy	1999
Ian Walker	2004

DID YOU KNOW THAT?

Three Leicester City players – Peter Shilton, Keith Weller and Frank Worthington – all played in the same England side against Scotland and Argentina in May 1974. A total of 16 Leicester City (including Leicester Fosse) players have been capped by England.

DID YOU KNOW THAT?

Two of England's three most capped goalkeepers, Peter Shilton (125) and Gordon Banks (73) began their careers at Leicester City. Banks was, of course, England's goalkeeper in the 1966 World Cup Final and he produced "the save of the century" to deny Pele a goal in the 1970 finals in Guadalajara, Mexico. An eye injury in a car crash ended Banks's career when he was still in his prime. Shilton was the England goalkeeper in the country's only other World Cup semi-final, the loss on penalties to West Germany in the 1990 competition in Italy.

England's Last 10 Notts Magpies

Player	Years
William Gunn	1884
John Dixon	1885
Charles Dobson	1886
Alfred Shelton	1889–92
Henry Daft	1889–92
George Toone	1892
Percy Humphreys	1903
Herbert Morley	1910
William Ashurst	1923–25
Tommy Lawton	1947–48

DID YOU KNOW THAT?

Notts County are one of the oldest football clubs in the world, formed in November 1862, and have provided players for England's national team since 1883. Three County players, Stuart Macrae, Arthur Cursham and Henry Cursham, played for England against Wales in the 5–0 win at the Kennington Oval on 3 February 1883. Notts County were a Football League Third Division side when Tommy Lawton signed for them, and then played for England. A total of 20 Notts County players have been capped by England.

DID YOU KNOW THAT?

Notts County play in the city of Nottingham, unlike their neighbours, Nottingham Forest, who play in West Bridgeford, on the other side of the River Trent. In 2009, former England coach Sven-Goran Eriksson was appointed Director of Football at Meadow Lane and one of the players to join County, albeit for only one match, was Sol Campbell.

England's Last 10 Pompey Boys

Player	Years
Jimmy Dickinson	1949–56
Peter Harris	1949–54
Jack Froggatt	1949–53
Len Phillips	1951–54
Mark Hateley	1984
David James	2007–present
Sol Campbell	2007–09
Glen Johnson	2007–09
Peter Crouch	2007–09
Jermain Defoe	2008–09

DID YOU KNOW THAT?

Two Pompey players started for England on several occasions throughout the late 1940s and early 1950s. The first time this occurred was when Jimmy Dickinson and Peter Harris played in England's 2–0 home defeat to Eire on 21 September 1949, England's first defeat to a foreign team on English soil. Jimmy Dickinson started alongside Jack Froggatt 12 times between 1949 and 1953. A total of 16 Portsmouth players have been capped by England.

DID YOU KNOW THAT?

When Jermain Defoe joined Portsmouth in 2008, Pompey had five current England internationals in their squad, their most for more than 50 years. In May that year, Portsmouth defeated Cardiff City 1–0 at Wembley to become the first club from a city other than London, Manchester or Liverpool to win the FA Cup for more than 20 years and it was the first FA Cup final of the 21st century without a London club in it.

England's Last 10 Potters

Player	Years
Freddie Steele	1936–37
Joe Johnson	1936–37
Neil Franklin	1946–50
Tony Allen	1959
Gordon Banks	1967–72
Mike Pejic	1974
Alan Hudson	1975
Peter Shilton	1977
Dave Watson	1982
Mark Chamberlain	1982–84

DID YOU KNOW THAT?

Three Stoke City players have started for England on two occasions. The first was in 1892 and the second on 17 April 1937 against Scotland in a 3–1 defeat at Hampden Park. Stanley Matthews, Joe Johnson and Freddie Steele all played that day, with Steele scoring for England. A total of 22 Stoke City players have been capped by England.

DID YOU KNOW THAT?

The greatest player in Stoke City's history was the legendary Stanley Matthews, but the club did not win a major trophy when he was with the club. In 1972, with Gordon Banks in goal for the Potters, Stoke City won the Football League Cup, beating Chelsea 2–1 in the Final. Another member of that Stoke team, and the scorer of the match-winning goal, was George Eastham, whose England career had ended while he was at Arsenal, but just a few months before he moved to the Midlands.

England's Last 10 Rams

Player	Years
Bert Mozley	1949
John Lee	1950
Roy McFarland	1971–76
Colin Todd	1972–77
David Nish	1973–74
Kevin Hector	1973
Charlie George	1977
Peter Shilton	1987–90
Mark Wright	1988–91
Seth Johnson	2001

DID YOU KNOW THAT?

Three Derby County players, George Kinsey, Stephen Bloomer and John Goodall, were in the England side that beat Wales 9–1 in Cardiff on 16 March 1896. Bloomer scored five times and Goodall once. A total of 38 Derby County players have been capped by England.

DID YOU KNOW THAT?

Derby County appointed former England international Nigel Clough as the club's new manager in January 2009. He was following in some pretty famous footsteps, being the son of Derby's most successful ever manager, Brian Clough. Clough senior developed long-time England stars, and centre-back partners, Roy McFarland and Colin Todd, and guided the Rams to the First Division Championship for the first time in club history in 1972. Both Todd and McFarland later were managers of the Rams, and the latter also succeeded Clough junior as manager of Burton Albion in 2009.

England's Last 10 Rangers

Player	Years
Dave Thomas	1974–75
Dave Clement	1976–77
John Gregory	1983–84
Terry Fenwick	1984–86
Clive Allen	1984
David Seaman	1988–90
Paul Parker	1989–91
Andy Sinton	1991–93
David Bardsley	1992–93
Les Ferdinand	1993–94

DID YOU KNOW THAT?
Only once have three Queens Park Rangers players ever started for England together. Gerry Francis, Ian Gillard and Dave Thomas all played in England's 2–2 draw against Wales at Wembley on 21 May 1975. Gerry Francis captained England in 1976 when they played a Team America side led by the legendary Bobby Moore. A total of 16 QPR players have been capped by England.

DID YOU KNOW THAT?
Former Rangers and England captain Gerry Francis had two spells as manager at Loftus Road. As skipper, Francis led the team to their best-ever finish in the Football League, second behind Liverpool in 1975–76. Rangers were a Third Division club when they won their first major trophy, the 1967 Football League Cup. Their star player at the time was Rodney Marsh, who won nine England caps with Rangers and Manchester City between 1971 and 1973.

England's Last 10 Rovers

Player	Years
Alan Shearer	1992–96
Stuart Ripley	1993–97
David Batty	1994–95
Tim Flowers	1994–98
Graeme Le Saux	1994–97
Jason Wilcox	1996–99
Chris Sutton	1997
David Dunn	2002
David Bentley	2007–08
Paul Robinson	2008–present

DID YOU KNOW THAT?

Five Blackburn Rovers players were in England's starting line-up when they beat Ireland 9–1 in Belfast on 15 March 1890: John Barton, James Forrest, Joe Lofthouse, Nat Walton and Bill Townley. Barton, Lofthouse and Townley all scored in the game. A total of 47 Blackburn players have been capped by England.

DID YOU KNOW THAT?

In the mid-1990s Blackburn Rovers were funded by Sir Jack Walker and as chairman he bankrolled the club to great success, culminating in the 1995 Premier League title, their first League title for 81 years. Spearheading the club on the pitch was centre-forward Alan Shearer, who was transferred to Newcastle United in 1996 for a then world record £15 million. Since winning the Premier League title, Rovers have never finished in the top five in the division and, indeed spent two seasons in what is now the Championship.

England's Last 10 Seasiders

Player	Years
Stanley Matthews	1947–57
Stan Mortensen	1947–53
Eddie Shimwell	1949
Tom Garrett	1952–53
Ernie Taylor	1953
William Perry	1955–56
Jimmy Armfield	1959–66
Ray Charnley	1962
Tony Waiters	1964
Alan Ball	1965–66

DID YOU KNOW THAT?

Four Blackpool players were in the starting 11 for England against Hungary on 25 November 1953 when "the Mighty Magyars" taught England a lesson, winning 6–3 at Wembley. Harry Johnston, Stan Matthews, Stan Mortensen and Ernie Taylor all played in the game. When Hungary beat England 7–1 in Budapest the following May not a single Blackpool player was on the pitch. A total of 13 Blackpool players have been capped by England.

DID YOU KNOW THAT?

Blackpool's glory days came in the years immediately after World War II, when the likes of Stanley Matthews and Stan Mortensen filled not only Bloomfield Road, but grounds around the country. Mortensen scored the only ever FA Cup Final hat-trick at the old Wembley Stadium in 1953, but he was overshadowed by the "Wizard of the Dribble" Matthews, who set up Bill Perry for the match-winner against Bolton.

England's Last 10 Toffees

Player	Years
Martin Keown	1992
David Unsworth	1995
Andy Hinchcliffe	1996–97
Nicky Barmby	2000
Michael Ball	2001
Wayne Rooney	2003–04
Phil Neville	2005–present
Andrew Johnson	2006–08
Joleon Lescott	2007–09
Phil Jagielka	2008–present

DID YOU KNOW THAT?

Four Everton players featured in the same England side against Poland, Paraguay and Argentina during the 1986 World Cup finals in Mexico. The four were Gary Stevens, Trevor Steven, Peter Reid and Gary Lineker. A total of 61 Everton players have been capped by England.

DID YOU KNOW THAT?

Goodison Park, Everton's home since 1893, was one of the 1966 World Cup venues and it was witness to the most remarkable game of those finals when Portugal came from 3–0 down to beat Italy's conquerors North Korea 5–3, with Eurebio scoring four times. The only Evertonian in England's World Cup-winning team was left-back Ramon Wilson, but he was soon joined by Alan Ball, who was transferred from Blackpool a few weeks after the Final. When he was a teenager, Phil Neville was considered the best young cricketer in Lancashire, better even than Andrew Flintoff.

England's Last 10 Wolves

Player	Years
Ron Flowers	1955–66
Eddie Clamp	1958
Peter Broadbent	1958–60
Norman Deeley	1959
Chris Crowe	1962
Alan Hinton	1962
Bobby Thomson	1963–64
John Richards	1973
Emlyn Hughes	1980
Steve Bull	1989–90

DID YOU KNOW THAT?

Four Wolverhampton Wanderers players, Billy Wright, Bert Williams, Ron Flowers and Dennis Wishaw, all started for England against France on 15 May 1955 when England lost 1–0 in Paris. Another four, Billy Wright, Ron Flowers, Norman Deeley and Peter Broadbent, started against Brazil in Rio de Janeiro on 13 May 1959, when England lost 2–0. A total of 33 Wolves players have been capped by England.

DID YOU KNOW THAT?

Billy Wright was the first England player to win 100 caps, and he shares with Bobby Moore the honour of having led the team on 90 occasions. The last Wolves player to captain England was Emlyn Hughes, who wore the armband against Northern Ireland on 20 May 1980, when he made his last start and penultimate appearance for his country. He had also skippered Wolves to victory in the 1980 League Cup, his first success in the competition.

CHAPTER
7

ENGLAND QUOTES

Let's be honest, if you ask any footballer for their thoughts as they walk off the pitch following a fantastic victory or demoralising defeat, you're not going to get an existentialist discourse on the vagaries of the bouncing ball and the capricious nature of inclement weather. Over the next few pages, you won't find "We're over the moon," or "erm, it was, you know, erm great," or, "I'm gutted for the boys."

Instead you will find around 50 quotes from the last half-century. These quotes, observations and comments come from players, managers and the media about the England team, their performances on and off the pitch, players and managers. Some are funny, some sad, many will be well known to most fans, but there are others that will come as a surprise.

Many of the funniest quotes come from people who forget the cardinal rule of public speaking: think first, speak second. Then again, the right words come out, but not necessarily in the right order. Others just try too hard, like the over-excited television commentator, who watched a golden opportunity being wasted and said, "He took the ball around the goalkeeper but literally lost his head and kicked it over the bar." That must have been messy!

1

"Some people are on the pitch ... they think it's all over ... it is now."

Kenneth Wolstenholme, *the famous BBC television commentary at the end of the 1966 World Cup Final.*

2

"Everybody went crazy, but I wasn't sure if it was a goal because the referee seemed to blow his whistle as the ball went in. When I realised it was a goal I was incredibly pleased."

Geoff Hurst, *talking about the goal to complete his World Cup Final hat-trick.*

3

"We were the world champions which was a fantastic feeling. I knew that life for me would never be the same again."

Bobby Charlton, *remembering English football's finest hour.*

4

"At the end of the Final I remember being absolutely drained. I've seen some photographs after the game and I look about 90."

Ray Wilson, *recalling exhaustion more than elation.*

5

"As we came round the corner from the 18th green, a crowd of members were at the clubhouse window cheering and waiting to tell me that England had won the World Cup. It was the blackest day of my life."

Denis Law, *recalling a day that not every Briton enjoyed.*

The Fourth Estate

1

"The end of the world"

The Sun's *headline after England had failed
to qualify for the 1974 World Cup.*

2

**"Eriksson should go because this man
has as good a chance of winning the World Cup
as I have of winning the London Marathon."**

David Mellor, *aged 56, pulling no punches
in a March 2005* Evening Standard *column.*

3

"In the name of Allah, go!"

The Sun, *again, this time demanding
Bobby Robson's departure following
a 1988 draw with Saudi Arabia.*

4

**"There have, of course, been worse moments in
English history – the Roman Conquest, the Black Death,
the Civil War, the fall of France in 1940 and
virtually the whole of the 1970s, for example."**

The Times *leader comment after England were
knocked out of the 2002 World Cup.*

5

"Yanks 2, Planks 0"

The Sun's *verdict after England lost
in the USA in 1993.*

A Spot of Bother

1

"With both penalties David Beckham snatched at the ball like an adolescent golfer teeing off in front of the clubhouse. The England captain choked."

Matthew Syed, The Times *correspondent,*
berating Becks after his Euro 2004 penalty misses.

2

"The good news is that Saddam Hussein is facing the death penalty. The bad news is that David Beckham is taking it!"

Cruel anonymous internet joke, 2004.

3

"I put the penalty where I wanted, but not far enough in the corner. When he saved it, there was just an incredible sense of deflation, a sense of: this really wasn't meant to happen."

Gareth Southgate, *on his Euro 96 penalty shoot-out miss.*

4

"Why didn't you just belt it, son?"
Barbara Southgate, Gareth's mum,
proving that mothers do know best!

5

"Mary and I got the shock of our lives when David was asked to take a penalty. Neither of us really expected David to score."
Al Batty, David's father after England lost
on penalties at France 98.

Glory Days

1

"At the time it was really special, especially against the Old Enemy. In Scotland, they try to erase the game from the memory; if you tried to talk about it, they'd change the subject."
Jimmy Armfield, *recalling England's 9–3 defeat of Scotland in 1961.*

2

"I could see Colin Hendry coming in, so I flicked it over his head and volleyed it. God, the feeling when I scored was magnificent! I'm so glad I scored that goal."
Paul Gascoigne *recalls his effort against Scotland in Euro 96.*

3

"I have no doubts whatsoever that Germany will thrash England and qualify easily for the World Cup. What could possibly go wrong? The English haven't beaten us in Munich for a hundred years."
Uli Hoeness *previews England's 2001 World Cup qualifier in Munich.*

4

"We all know we've made history tonight. We all know we are part of something special."
Steven Gerrard *proves Herr Hoeness slightly wrong!*

5

"The 5–1 defeat by England was like the explosion of a nuclear bomb. The scars will last for life."
Oliver Kahn, *the man who conceded those five goals, suffering from football hyperbole.*

The Poisoned Chalice

1

*"At last England have appointed a man who speaks
English better than the players."*
Brian Clough *on Sven-Goran Eriksson.*

2

*"I just feel I fall a little short of what is required for this job.
I sat there in the first half and could see things weren't right
but I couldn't find it in myself to solve the problem."*
Kevin Keegan *resigns as England manager, September 2000.*

3

*"Hoddle's attitude betrays a disabled mind.
It seems he has no compassion, no allowance for weakness."*
Ian Dury, *singer and actor, reacts to Glenn Hoddle's 1999 comments
about disability being karma working from another lifetime.
Hoddle resigned soon after.*

4

*"Football is a simple game.
The hard part is making it look simple."*
Ron Greenwood, *England manager, 1978.*

5

"I used to quite like turnips. Now my wife refuses to serve them."
Graham Taylor, *reflecting on his England team being called turnips
after losing to Sweden in Euro 92.*

Argy Bargy

1

"England's best football will come against the right type of opposition – a team who come to play football and not act as animals."

Alf Ramsey, *talking after the World Cup 1966 quarter-final.*

2

"A little bit the hand of God, a little the head of Diego."

Diego Maradona, *describing his first goal against England in 1986.*

3

"It wasn't the hand of God. It was the hand of a rascal. God had nothing to do with it."

Bobby Robson, *England manager, has a slight different perspective.*

4

"As for Maradona's second goal, well, that was something special. All I saw was the back of him running, this number ten steaming down the pitch."

Kenny Sansom, *one of the six England players beaten on his mazy run.*

5

"There's one thing I can say without fear of contradiction: I know I couldn't have buried it any better."

Michael Owen *on his wonder goal against Argentina in 1998.*

Modern Legends

1

"I want more from David Beckham.
I want him to improve on perfection."
Kevin Keegan, *2000.*

2

"I don't remember anyone making such an impact
on a tournament since Pele in the 1958 World Cup."
Sven-Goran Eriksson, *on 18-year-old Wayne Rooney after Euro 2004.*

3

"I honestly believe we have a great chance
of winning the World Cup next summer."
John Terry *gets it wrong in 2005. Maybe he was four years out!*

4

"Michael Owen is a goalscorer –
not a natural born one, not yet, that takes time."
Glenn Hoddle, *England coach,*
just before Owen made a spectacular impact on France 98.

5

"Nobby Stiles once told me that he thought Steven Gerrard
was the nearest thing to Duncan Edwards and that's
a tremendous compliment. His all-action displays constantly
put pressure on the opposition and he must be the best
midfielder in the world at present."
Tommy Smith, *former Liverpool legend,*
in 2004 on a current Liverpool legend.

Say What You Mean

1

"Lord Nelson, Lord Beaverbrook, Sir Winston Churchill, Sir Anthony Eden, Clement Attlee, Henry Cooper, Lady Diana, Maggie Thatcher. Can you hear me, Maggie Thatcher? Your boys took a helluva beating. Norway has beaten England at football!"

Burge Lillelien, *Norwegian football commentator,*
after England lost 2–1 to Norway in a 1981 World Cup qualifier.

2

"In the studio, Des Lynam's line-up of pundits resembled an evolutionary wall-chart of human articulacy, starting with Paul Gascoigne at the primeval end and peaking, surprisingly, with Gary Neville."

David Bennun, Mail on Sunday *TV critic,*
reviewing ITV's coverage of England vs Denmark in 2002.

3

"You've beaten them once. Now go out and bloody beat them again."

Alf Ramsey, *to the England team before extra-time in the 1966 World Cup Final.*

4

"I do want to play the short ball and I do want to play the long ball. I think long and short balls is what football is all about."

Bobby Robson, *England manager, explaining his football policy.*

5

"Football is a simple game. Twenty-two men chase a ball for 90 minutes and, in the end, the Germans win."

Gary Lineker, *taking a jaundiced view of matches from 1968 to 2001.*

Road to South Africa

1

"I played with one less stud. My boot went to bits and I was going to change, but the boots wouldn't have suited me."
Theo Walcott, *noting his damaged footwear didn't stop him from scoring a hat-trick in Croatia in 2008.*

2

"England showed they are a mighty team, probably the best in Europe."
Slaven Bilic, *after his Croatia team had been beaten 4–1 at home in September 2008.*

3

"It meant a lot and it has given us the win, so I'm delighted. There was some great fight and desire from the lads."
John Terry, *on scoring the match-winner against Ukraine at Wembley.*

4

"I think he can go on holiday. He scored a goal, he signed a new contract and he changed his team. It's been a fantastic weekend for him."
Fabio Capello *talking about Gareth Barry being suspended following his goal and booking in the 4–0 win over Kazakhstan.*

5

"We've got a long way to go to win the whole thing, obviously, but we've qualified and we're there."
Frank Lampard, *after England had beaten Croatia 5–1 to qualify for South Africa.*

His Master's Voice

1

"He made one mistake, that is all,
and that was for the penalty.
The only other one was for the goal."
Fabio Capello, *England coach, on Rio Ferdinand's*
unhappy evening in Ukraine, 2009.
Something lost in translation, boss?

2

"He'll pull you up in front of the lads in team meetings,
rewind things and say: 'Look at that.'
He's on top of every small detail."
John Terry *praises his manager's eagle-eyed*
review of matches, 2009.

3

"I don't know how I got that. Thanks, Brucie."
David Beckham *reacts to Steve Bruce naming him man of the match*
against Belarus in October 2009, despite being on the pitch
for just over half an hour.

4

"It is like Barack Obama winning the Nobel peace prize
after nine months as President."
Fabio Capello *is equally surprised at Mr Bruce's decision.*

5

"Fabio Capello makes managing England look easy."
Phil McNulty, *BBC Sport blogger, October 2009.*

CHAPTER

8

ENGLAND SONGS & CHANTS

Football fans love a good sing-song and this chapter will help you with the all-important words to go with the tunes. We're sure you know the words to the National Anthem, but just in case you don't, we've included it. You'll also find the words to football's favourite hymn, "Abide with Me", and to other great England standards, including "Rule Britannia" and "Land of Hope and Glory".

But it isn't just the fans who do the singing; the players have been known to cut the odd (very odd some might say) record. Whether it was John Barnes rapping away with the England squad in 1990 with New Order's "World in Motion" or the altogether less successful "Fog on the Tyne" featuring Paul Gascoigne, you can recall all the chart hits and misses involving either the whole squad or just odd members.

Every fan has their favourite chant, but most are about clubs or, less flatteringly, their opponents. Most of these shouldn't be heard, let alone printed, and few translate to the national team. However, we have included the lyrics for a few of the chants which every England fan should know well (and the tunes from which they're taken). So, stand up, take a deep breath and … "Inger-land, Inger-land, Inger land, Inger-land."

God Save the Queen

God save our gracious Queen,
Long live our noble Queen,
God save the Queen.
Send her victorious,
Happy and glorious,
Long to reign over us,
God save the Queen.

DID YOU KNOW THAT?
The music for "God Save the Queen" is the same for *Oben am Jungen Rhein* (Up Above the Young Rhine), the national anthem of Liechtenstein.

Land of Hope and Glory

Land of Hope and Glory,
Mother of the Free,
How shall we extol thee,
Who are born of thee?
Wider still and wider
Shall thy bounds be set,
God, who made thee mighty,
Make thee mightier yet,
God, who made thee mighty,
Make thee mightier yet.

DID YOU KNOW THAT?
"Land of Hope and Glory" is always the last song performed at the BBC's "Last Night of the Proms". It brings down the curtain on the eight-week-long annual classical music festival, which was originally called "The Henry Wood Promenade Concerts".

Jerusalem

And did those feet in ancient time
Walk upon England's mountains green
And was the holy lamb of God
On England's pleasant pastures seen.

And did the countenance divine
Shine forth upon our clouded hills
And was Jerusalem builded here
Among those dark Satanic mills.

Bring me my bow of burning gold
Bring me my arrows of desire
Bring me my spears o'clouds unfold
Bring me my chariot of fire.

I will not cease from mental fight
Nor shall my sword sleep in my hand
'Til we have built Jerusalem
In England's green and pleasant land
'Til we have built Jerusalem
In England's green and pleasant land.

From the poem by William Blake

DID YOU KNOW THAT?

William Blake's famous poem, "And did those feet in ancient time", is better known today as the patriotic hymn "Jerusalem". Blake was inspired to write the poem, a preface to his early-19th-century work, *Milton: A Poem*, after reading the story of a young Jesus Christ, travelling with his uncle, Joseph of Arimathea, to an area which today is thought to be somewhere close to Glastonbury in Gloucestershire, England.

Swing Low, Sweet Chariot

Swing low, sweet chariot,
Coming for to carry me home.
Swing low, sweet chariot,
Coming for to carry me home.

I looked over Jordan and what did I see,
Coming for to carry me home ?
A band of angels coming after me,
Coming for to carry me home.

DID YOU KNOW THAT?
The first recording of this Negro spiritual hymn was in 1909.
England adopted it for the 1991 Rugby Union World Cup.

Abide with Me

Abide with me!
Fast falls the eventide,
The darkness deepens
Lord, with me abide!
When other helpers fail
And comforts flee,
Help of the helpless,
Oh, abide with me!

DID YOU KNOW THAT?
"Abide with Me" was first sung at an FA Cup Final in
1927, the year the trophy left England for the first and, to
date, only time when Cardiff City caused a sensation
by beating Arsenal 1–0. The hymn has been sung before the
kick-off to every FA Cup Final since.

Rule, Britannia

Rule, Britannia!
Britannia, rule the waves!
Britons never, never, never
Shall be slaves.

DID YOU KNOW THAT?
John Lennon of the Beatles sings part of "Rule, Britannia" in the film *A Hard Day's Night*.

Inger-land

Inger-land, Inger-land, Inger-land,
Inger-land, Inger-land, Inger-land,
Inger-land, Inger-land, Inger-land,
Inger-land.

Ten German Bombers

There were ten German bombers in the air,
There were ten German bombers in the air,
There were ten German bombers,
Ten German bombers,
There were ten German bombers in the air,
And the RAF from England shot one down,
And the RAF from England shot one down,
And the RAF from England, the RAF from England,
And the RAF from England shot one down.

Repeat in descending order of number of German bombers.

Theme from *The Great Escape*

Da-da da-da da
Da-da, da-da da
Da-da, da-da da-da da-da dah
Da-da da-da da
Da-da, da-da da
Da-da da-da da-da da dah.
England!

DID YOU KNOW THAT?

"The Great Escape" was a mass escape attempt from Stalag Luft III, a Nazi-run prisoner of war camp in Poland on 24 March 1944. Only three of the 76 escapees made it back to England.

Two World Wars and One World Cup

Two World Wars and One World Cup
Two World Wars and One World Cup
England, England.
Two World Wars and One World Cup
England, England …

Sung to the tune of the "Camptown Races".

Keep St George in My Heart

Keep St George in my Heart, keep me English,
Keep St George in my Heart I pray.
Keep St George in my Heart, keep me English,
Keep me English till my dying day

We Love You England

We love you England,
We do.
We love you England
We do.
We love you England
We do.
Oh England, we love you.

Oh When the Saints Go Marching In

Oh, when the saints go marching in,
Oh, when the saints go marching in,
I want to be in that number,
When the saints go marching in.
England!

Theme from *The Dambusters*

Darr da da, da da-da da da da
Da da da da-da da da-da
Da-da da da da-da
Da da da-da da darr
England!

DID YOU KNOW THAT?

There will be no official England World Cup song at the 2010 World Cup finals. Coach Fabio Capello wants to keep the squad focused on football. He also insisted that the players' WAGs will have a much lower profile than in 2006.

CHAPTER

9

ENGLAND QUIZZES & PUZZLES

So you think you know all about the England team? Well, over the next few pages you will find out if it's true or not. Not only are there ten pub-quiz-style questions each about England internationals, players, matches and tournaments, but there are a couple of crosswords and teasing word searches and tricky conundrums too.

A dedicated, older football fan, or at least one who loves taking part in pub quizzes, will probably have little trouble in answering the vast majority of the quiz questions. As well as some general rounds on England, there are a couple that focus on the World Cup. The questions have three levels of difficulty: easy, medium and hard. The easy questions are just that, meant to build up your confidence. After that the medium questions will get you thinking but aren't too tough. Finally we have the difficult rounds and these are what they say on the label, "difficult" with a capital D.

As for the other puzzles, they are self-explanatory. The crosswords have no cryptic clues and the other ones don't require great knowledge, just a logical mind.

And, because we're kind, generous souls, we've given you all the answers.

Quiz 1: Three Lions 1

1 Which club was Steve Stone with when he made his international debut?
2 Which player scored England's first goal in Euro 96?
3 Who is England's all-time record goalscorer?
4 Which 20-year-old winger scored a wonder goal for England in Brazil in 1984?
5 Which England forward Peter's career was from 1986 to 1996?
6 Terry Butcher and Paul Mariner were colleagues at which club?
7 Who was England's first-choice goalkeeper in the 1990 World Cup in Italy?
8 What is the first name of 80s striker Blissett?
9 Who was known as "The Wizard of the Dribble"?
10 Who was in tears after the World Cup semi-final defeat in 1990?
11 Who scored for England in their record defeat by Hungary in 1954?
12 What forename was shared by Francis and Brooking?
13 Which club did Ronnie Clayton play for?
14 Which club was Bobby Moore with when he became England captain?
15 Which Liverpool full-back made his international debut aged 20?
16 Which David made his debut against Moldova?
17 Which Kenny made 86 appearances at full-back?
18 Which striker hit five goals in one game in the 70s?
19 Which club was Steve Coppell with during his international career?
20 What forename links Bull and McManaman?
21 Whose back pass became an own goal when England lost 2–0 to Croatia in 2007?
22 Who were England's first opponents at the new Wembley Stadium?
23 What was the result of England's last Euro 2008 qualifying match?
24 Which Caribbean team did England play in the summer of 2006 and 2008?
25 Who scored England's last goal of the 2006 World Cup finals?

Quiz 2: England Managers

1 Which England manager was born in Worksop?

2 How many games did Joe Mercer serve as caretaker manager?

3 Which was Alf Ramsey's first club as a player?

4 Who were the opponents in Terry Venables's first game as boss?

5 How many of manager Don Revie's 29 England matches ended in defeat?

6 Which manager accused his players of "running round like headless chickens"?

7 Walter Winterbottom led England into how many World Cups?

8 How many England caps did Bobby Robson win as a player?

9 For how many games was Alf Ramsey in charge of England?

10 Which manager had his biggest victory in his last game?

11 Who formed a management partnership with Joe Mercer at Coventry in the 1970s?

12 Who was made skipper in Terry Venables's first game in charge?

13 Ron Greenwood's 1982 World Cup campaign was marred by injuries to which two key players?

14 Who scored for England in the Swedes 2 v Turnips 1 game?

15 Which England manager has won most World Cup games?

16 Where was Walter Winterbottom born?

17 Including penalty shoot-outs, who scored the last England goal under Terry Venables?

18 Which club did Ron Greenwood become a director of in 1983?

19 Who scored the last England goal for Graham Taylor?

20 How many England managers did Kevin Keegan play for?

21 Before 2009, who was the last England manager to resign?

22 Which former England manager, in 2005, was posthumously inducted into the English Football Hall of Fame?

23 Which ex-England coach played for two Lincolnshire Senior Cup-winning clubs?

24 For which club did Steve McClaren play in season 1988–89?

25 Which England manager died on 9 February 2006, aged 84, after a long struggle with Alzheimer's disease?

Quiz 3: World Cup

1 How far did England advance to in the 1990 World Cup?
2 Who scored in the first minute against France in the 1982?
3 Whose two goals knocked out England in 1986?
4 Who won the Golden Boot for most goals in the 1986 World Cup?
5 Which England keeper was known as Shilts?
6 Which influential player did Sir Alf Ramsey substitute when England were winning 2–0 against West Germany in Mexico 70?
7 Which African nation did England beat in the 1990 quarter-final?
8 Who scored England's penalty against Argentina in 1998?
9 Who managed England during the 1986 and 1990 World Cups?
10 From which World Cup did England exit after penalty misses by Stuart Pearce and Chris Waddle?
11 Who was accused of stealing a bracelet prior to Mexico 70?
12 Where did England play Argentina in France 98?
13 Who cried after being booked against Germany in 1990?
14 Who "golden goal" was disallowed against Argentina in France 98?
15 Which South American nation did England beat in the 1998 finals?
16 Which England goalkeeper made "the save of the century" against Brazil in Mexico 70?
17 Which then-Chelsea player scored Romania's winner against England in 1998?
18 Who scored with a last-minute volley against Belgium in 1990?
19 In which year did England play France, Czechoslovakia, Kuwait, West Germany and Spain?
20 Which goal in the 1966 Final was confirmed by a linesman?
21 In how many World Cup finals did Bryan Robson appear?
22 At which club was Jack Charlton when he won the World Cup?
23 How many players were in both of England's 1998 and 2006 World Cup squads?
24 Which club had seven representatives on the pitch at the end of a qualifying game in Albania in 2001?
25 Which keeper went to the 2002 and 06 finals, but didn't play in a single match?

Quiz 4: England Heroes

1 Who was England's hat-trick hero in the 1966 World Cup Final?
2 Who is England's all-time top scorer?
3 Who scored 48 international goals before becoming a TV presenter?
4 Which former England hero Kevin became the manager?
5 Who played the first of his 84 matches for England in 1934?
6 Who won his 106th and last cap against West Germany in 1970?
7 Which England player was known as "Captain Marvel"?
8 Which England player was leading scorer at Euro 96?
9 Which 1950s England hero was married to a Beverley Sister?
10 Who scored England's equaliser in the Italia 90 semi-final?
11 Who is England's youngest-ever goalscorer?
12 Who was regarded as England's best player during Euro 2000?
13 Who was England's goalkeeping hero against Scotland in Euro 96?
14 What made him a hero in that game?
15 Who scored all three goals against Poland in the 1986 finals?
16 Who scored for England against Belgium in the second-round match in Italia 90?
17 Which Londoner scored 44 goals in 57 appearances for England during the 1960s?
18 Which England hero played his last international against Italy at Wembley in November 1973?
19 Who retired from international football after Euro 2000?
20 Who scored England's second goal against Portugal in their Euro 2000 opener?
21 In which city did Theo Walcott score an England hat-trick in a World Cup 2010 qualifier?
22 Who became England's most capped outfield player in 2009?
23 Which England sub scored the team's second goal against Sweden in the 2006 World Cup?
24 Which England star was his team's top goalscorer in 2009 but also suffered relegation?
25 Which England skipper was the match winner against Ukraine at Wembley in April 2009?

Quiz 5: Three Lions 2

1 David Seaman was at which club when he won his first full cap?
2 Who played his first England game in 1935 and his last in 1957?
3 How many times did Brian Little play for England?
4 Which two players in England's 1986 World Cup squad had the same name?
5 What links Alan Shearer, Robert Lee and Dennis Wise's debuts?
6 Gary Lineker played his last game against which country?
7 How many hat-tricks did Geoff Hurst score for England?
8 Who began his international career by scoring 2, 3, 2, 2, 3?
9 Who was England's first black player in a full international?
10 Who was voted best defender in the world by journalists after the 1970 World Cup?
11 Steve McManaman first came on as a sub in November 1994, against which country?
12 Which club was Mark Walters with when he made his only England appearance?
13 In September 1987 who became the 1,000th England player?
14 Who hit his first England hat-trick in the 7–1 San Marino romp?
15 Who played left wing, right wing and centre-forward and hit 30 goals?
16 Who scored 9 goals in 10 England matches in season 1992–93?
17 Who was left-back in the 1966 World Cup-winning side?
18 Who is the most capped Hughes to play for England?
19 To five each way, how many full England caps did Ray Wilkins win?
20 Which full-back has listed "Anarchy in the UK" by the Sex Pistols as his favourite musical track?
21 Which England captain led a Football League-winning club in three different decades?
22 On 15 December 1982, who became the first black player to score for England in a full international?
23 How many Everton players were in England's Mexico 1986 squad?
24 Which ex-Southampton and Manchester United winger won his only cap and scored against Egypt in 1986?
25 Against which country was Robert Green sent off in October 2009?

Quiz 6: England Pot Luck

1   Who did England play in their final 2010 World Cup qualifier?
2   What was the score in England's biggest win in a 2010 qualifier?
3   Who scored England's first hat-trick in the 2010 qualifiers?
4   Which World Cup semi-finalists did England beat 5–1 in 2008?
5   Which country hosted England's 2002 World Cup finals matches?
6   Excluding England, how many countries have won the World Cup?
7   When did England first lose to European opponents?
8   When did England first lose at Wembley to European opponents?
9   Which World Cup 2010 qualifier was not broadcast live on TV?
10 Which former England manager died in August 2009?
11 Who were England's last Home International Championship opponents?
12 In which city did England play Andorra in September 2008?
13 Against whom did England lose their first match after winning the World Cup in 1966?
14 Where did England play their first ever home games?
15 Where was England's abandoned match against the Republic of Ireland in Feburary 1995?
16 What was the score in England's last qualifier for Euro 2008?
17 Who was England's goalkeeping coach under Ericksson, McClaren and Capello?
18 Which goalkeeper conceded two penalties against Malta in 2000?
19 Where was England's first match in the Euro 2000 finals?
20 Who scored two penalties for England in 2010 qualifying games?
21 Name four of the five full England internationals since 1960 whose surnames contained only three letters?
22 Which of these England stars was never captain at senior level: Gordon Banks, Peter Beardsley, Bobby Charlton, David Seaman?
23 Who went in goal after Robert Green was sent off in 2009?
24 Which Blackpool player was in the 1966 World Cup-winning XI?
25 In which country did England play Brazil in a 2009 friendly?

Quiz 7: World Cup 2

1 When did England first take part in the World Cup finals?
2 Who embarrassingly defeated England in the 1950 finals?
3 What was the score when England were shocked in 1950?
4 In which country did England first play in the World Cup finals?
5 Who beat England in the quarter-finals of the 1954 tournament?
6 Who were England's first opponents in the 1966 finals?
7 Who did England beat in the semi final in 1966?
8 What was the score in England's 1966 semi-final?
9 England played Brazil in the group stages of the 1970 competition. What was the score?
10 How many wins did England have in the first group stage of the 1982 tournament?
11 England played a second-round match in 1982 against which South American team?
12 Where did England finish in Italia 90?
13 Who lost to England in the World Cup 1990 round of 16 match?
14 What was the score in the match that took England to the 1990 quarter-finals?
15 Who did England play in their opening game in the 1998 finals?
16 Who scored England's second goal in their France 98 opener?
17 Which country beat England in 90 minutes in the 1990 finals?
18 Which future regular England captain scored in the 1998 group stage?
19 What was the 90-minute score in England's 2006 quarter-final?
20 In which city did England go out of the 2006 World Cup?
21 Who was the first man to take England to consecutive World Cup finals after Sir Alf Ramsey?
22 Where and when was the first post-World War II World Cup finals for which England failed to qualify?
23 Which is the only country in which England have played in two World Cup finals?
24 Who won the Golden Boot at the 1986 finals?
25 Which 1980s finals was Trevor Brooking and Kevin Keegan's last?

Quiz 8: England Captains

1 Who is the only England captain to lift the World Cup trophy?

2 Which Wolves centre-half led England in 90 of his 105 games?

3 Who was the first black player to captain England?

4 Who led England during Euro 2000?

5 Who led England to six straight wins October 1960 to May 1961?

6 Which Arsenal player led England during the "Battle of Highbury" against Italy in 1934?

7 Who did Terry Venables name as his England captain for Euro 96?

8 Who captained England in the 1986 World Cup finals in Mexico?

9 Who took over as captain for the infamous match against Argentina in the same tournament?

10 Which goalkeeper led England during wartime internationals and two after the war?

11 Which England captain later became the team manager?

12 Which "Crazy Horse" captained England during the 1970s?

13 Who led England before Bobby Moore took over in 1963?

14 Who scored twice as skipper against Israel in February 1986?

15 Which Chelsea brother went on to captain England in the 1980s?

16 Which Ipswich full-back led England during the early 80s?

17 Which QPR midfielder led England eight times in the 1970s?

18 Who succeed injured team-mate Moore as captain in 1973–74?

19 How many times did Bobby Charlton skipper England?

20 Which Wolves player captained England in their 10–0 win over the USA in 1964?

21 Who was the youngest man to be named captain of England for a full international?

22 How old was Peter Shilton when he was captain against Italy in the 1990 World Cup third-place play-off match: 40, 41 or 42?

23 Which captain scored in his last two internationals at Euro 2000?

24 Name two of the four players to captain England during their 2003 defeat of Serbia and Montenegro.

25 Who succeeded David Beckham as England captain in 2006?

Quiz 9: Three Lions 3

1 How many goals did Stanley Matthews score for England?
2 Bobby Charlton's first England goal was against who?
3 Which player was outjumped by Pele before Banks made his save in Mexico 1970?
4 Which Brighton striker's only England appearance lasted eight minutes?
5 How many caps did Jimmy Greaves win after the 1966 World Cup?
6 Who was the first player to score 30 goals for England?
7 Gary Lineker missed a penalty against which country in 1992?
8 To two each way, how many caps did Glenn Hoddle win?
9 In how many games was Bobby Moore skipper of England?
10 Rodney Marsh was capped while at which two clubs?
11 Who scored for both sides in England's friendly v Holland in 1988?
12 How many games did Billy Wright miss between his first and last appearance for England?
13 Who was capped for England while at Werder Bremen in 1980?
14 Kenny Sansom won his last England cap in which tournament?
15 Who, in a 1962 World Cup game, picked up a dog which urinated on him?
16 To five each way, how many minutes was Kevin Hector on the field for his two England appearances?
17 How many caps did Gordon Banks win?
18 Timed at 17 seconds in 1947, who scored England's fastest goal?
19 In what year did Peter Shilton first play for England?
20 Which striker won six England full caps but did not score a goal?
21 Who was the last man to be sent off under Sven-Goran Eriksson?
22 Who is the only England player to score in three consecutive World Cup finals?
23 What was Michael Owen's number at France 98?
24 Who, at 31, was the old man of England's World Cup 2006 squad?
25 Who scored the last England goal while Steve McClaren was coach?

Quiz 10: England in Europe

1 Who were England's first opponents in the Euro 2000 finals?
2 What was the score in that match?
3 Who were the only team beaten by England in those finals?
4 Who scored England's winning goal in that match?
5 Who beat England in the semi-final of Euro 96?
6 Who were England's first opponents in the Euro 96 finals?
7 What was the score in that match?
8 Who scored England's second goal against Scotland at Wembley in Euro 96?
9 Who saved a penalty for England in that same match?
10 Who scored England's first goal in the Euro 2000 finals?
11 Who was England's manager during Euro 96?
12 Who did England play in the quarter-finals of Euro 96?
13 The quarter-finals of Euro 96 were played at Wembley, Villa Park, Anfield and which other ground?
14 England's Euro 96 group featured Scotland, Switzerland and which other country?
15 Who beat England in the final group match of Euro 2000?
16 Who gave away a penalty in that same match?
17 Which was the only team to beat England in Euro 92?
18 What was the score in that match?
19 Who scored the winning goal?
20 Which rule was introduced in the quarter-finals of Euro 96?
21 What country knocked England out of the 2004 European Championship finals?
22 Who scored England's penalty in their 1–0 win over Germany at Euro 2000?
23 At which European Championships did Peter Shilton earn his 100th England cap?
24 Which former Euro champions beat England 2–1 thanks to two late goals in a group game at Euro 2004?
25 Which two countries beat England 3–2 at Euro 2000?

All Letter Wordsearch

In the grid below you will find the 31 players England used in qualifying for the 2010 World Cup finals. They are written in a straight line, forward, back, up, down or on a diagonal line. Some are the full names, others are only first names and the rest only surnames. When you have found all of them, the unused letters will spell out something close to England hearts. What is missing?

S	J	G	A	R	E	T	H	B	A	R	R	Y	W	R
T	A	E	L	O	C	Y	E	L	H	S	A	T	R	J
E	G	R	Y	R	R	E	T	N	H	O	J	T	I	D
W	I	R	C	E	N	E	L	O	C	A	A	O	G	R
A	E	A	A	O	W	M	W	W	S	S	M	C	H	A
R	L	R	R	F	O	I	A	H	E	E	E	S	T	P
T	K	D	R	E	R	L	L	M	B	M	S	E	P	M
D	A	V	I	D	B	E	C	K	H	A	M	L	H	A
O	R	L	C	U	Y	H	O	E	C	J	I	N	I	L
W	R	O	K	Y	P	E	T	Y	U	E	L	O	L	K
N	I	S	O	N	T	S	T	N	O	N	N	E	L	N
I	O	U	E	N	A	K	O	D	R	A	E	L	I	A
N	N	L	I	U	E	E	M	N	C	S	R	O	P	R
G	G	R	E	E	N	Y	A	W	J	O	E	J	S	F
F	O	S	T	E	R	O	H	A	L	N	O	B	G	A

GABRIEL AGBONLAHOR
GARETH BARRY
DAVID BECKHAM
WAYNE BRIDGE
WES BROWN
MICHAEL CARRICK
ASHLEY COLE
CARLTON COLE
JOE COLE
PETER CROUCH
JERMAIN DEFOE

STEWART DOWNING
RIO FERDINAND
BEN FOSTER
STEVEN GERRARD
ROBERT GREEN
EMILE HESKEY
PHIL JAGIELKA
DAVID JAMES
JERMAINE JENAS
GLEN JOHNSON
FRANK LAMPARD

AARON LENNON
JOLEON LESCOTT
JAMES MILNER
WAYNE ROONEY
JOHN TERRY
MATTHEW UPSON
THEO WALCOTT
SHAUN WRIGHT-PHILLIPS
ASHLEY YOUNG

England World Cup Crossword 1

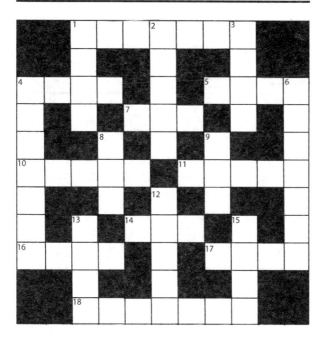

ACROSS

1 England's Italian coach Fabio *(7)*
4 The target for every striker *(4)*
5 English referee, Howard, with no hair *(4)*
7 Scouts do this on the next opponents *(3)*
10 Ex-West Brom and England striker from the 1970s, "Big" Cyrille *(5)*
11 Midfielder Lampard *(5)*
14 What you can't see in a domed stadium *(3)*
16 A match which ends with the scores level *(4)*
17 The eleven on pitch *(4)*
18 World Cup winners in 1966 and 2010 *(7)*

DOWN

1 What you do when your team scores *(4)*
2 Top African country, home of the Pyramids *(5)*
3 After 90 minutes, the game is this *(4)*
4 Steven is an England legend *(7)*
6 England's most capped outfield player *(7)*
8 You have to be this to play *(3)*
9 Only a goalkeeper can use this limb *(3)*
12 What international players have plenty of *(5)*
13 "The Beautiful ----" *(4)*
15 What *6 down* does to the ball like few others *(4)*

England World Cup Crossword 2

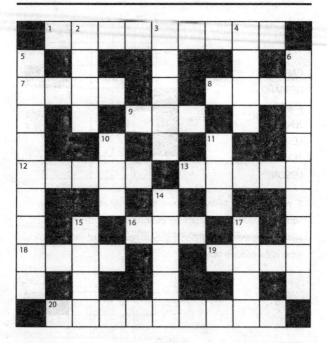

ACROSS

1 England defender with Brazilian first name *(9)*
7 Only three of the substitutes may be this *(4)*
8 Sign of an old injury *(4)*
9 35 is this in football age *(3)*
12 Don, 1950s England player, 1970s England manager *(5)*
13 First name of ex-England boss, Toon hero *(5)*
16 What all footballers are *(3)*
18 It is said that Capello rules with a rod of this *(4)*
19 England striker Collymore *(4)*
20 England's former captain and central defender *(4, 5)*

DOWN

2 "We'll support you .... more" *(4)*
3 World Cup winners in 2006 *(5)*
4 Former England star Barmby *(4)*
5 Oceania World Cup finalists in 2006, Asian finalists in 2010 *(9)*
6 South American giants, 1986 World Cup winners *(9)*
10 What all footballers want to do in every game *(3)*
11 First name of England goalkeeper Foster *(3)*
14 Time of day when floodlights will be used *(5)*
15 African country at World Cup finals in 2006 *(4)*
17 The best player in the team *(4)*

Staircase Conundrums 1/2

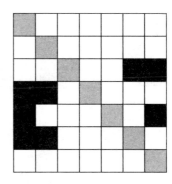

1

CARRICK
GERRARD
JAMES
JENAS
LESCOTT
TERRY
UPSON

If you enter the seven England players, all who have been in squads for 2010 qualifiers, into the grid in the correct order you will find another one written in the diagonal line of shaded boxes. Who is the hidden player?

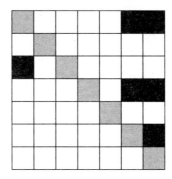

2

BARRY
BECKHAM
BULLARD
CROUCH
GREEN
LAMPARD
MILNER

If you enter the seven England players, all of whom have been called into squads since August 2008, into the grid in the correct order you will find another one written in the diagonal line of shaded boxes. Who is the hidden player?

Staircase Conundrums 3/4

3

BELGIUM
DENMARK
FINLAND
GEORGIA
GREECE
SWEDEN
TURKEY

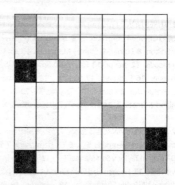

If you enter England's World Cup opponents from the last five tournaments, qualifying or finals, into the grid in the correct order you will find another one written in the diagonal line of shaded boxes. Which is the hidden country?

4

Alan BALL
David BECKHAM
Emlyn HUGHES
Paul INCE
Gary LINEKER
Stuart PEARCE
John TERRY

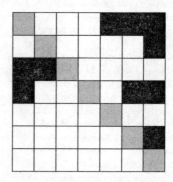

If you enter surnames of the seven England captains into the grid in the correct order you will find another one written in the diagonal line of shaded boxes. Who is the hidden skipper?

Answers

QUIZ 1: *THREE LIONS 1 (page 174)* **1** Nottingham Forest. **2** Alan Shearer.
3 Bobby Charlton. **4** John Barnes. **5** Beardsley. **6** Ipswich Town.
7 Peter Shilton. **8** Luther. **9** Stanley Matthews. **10** Paul Gascoigne.
11 Ivor Broadis. **12** Trevor. **13** Blackburn Rovers. **14** West Ham Utd.
15 Rob Jones. **16** Beckham. **17** Sansom. **18** Malcolm Macdonald.
19 Manchester Utd. **20** Steve. **21** Gary Neville. **22** Brazil.
23 England 2, Croatia 3. **24** Trinidad & Tobago. **25** David Beckham.

QUIZ 2: *ENGLAND MANAGERS (page 175)* **1** Graham Taylor. **2** Seven.
3 Southampton. **4** Denmark. **5** 7. **6** Graham Taylor. **7** Four. **8** 20.
9 3. **10** Graham Taylor, v San Marino 7–1. **11** Gordon Milne.
12 David Platt. **13** Keegan and Brooking. **14** David Platt. **15** Bobby Robson.
16 Oldham. **17** Teddy Sheringham. **18** Brighton. **19** Ian Wright.
20 Four. **21** Kevin Keegan. **22** Sir Walter Winterbottom.
23 Graham Taylor. **24** Bristol City. **25** Ron Greenwood.

QUIZ 3: *WORLD CUP 1 (page 176)* **1** Third-place playoff. **2** Bryan Robson.
3 Diego Maradona. **4** Gary Lineker. **5** Peter Shilton. **6** Bobby Charlton.
7 Cameroon. **8** Alan Shearer. **9** Bobby Robson. **10** 1990. **11** Bobby Moore.
12 St Etienne. **13** Paul Gascoigne. **14** Sol Campbell. **15** Colombia.
16 Gordon Banks. **17** Dan Petrescu. **18** David Platt. **19** 1982. **20** The third.
21 Three. **22** Leeds United. **23** Five. **24** Manchester United. **25** David James.

QUIZ 4: *ENGLAND HEROES (page 177)* **1** Geoff Hurst. **2** Bobby Charlton.
3 Gary Lineker. **4** Kevin Keegan. **5** Stanley Matthews. **6** Bobby Charlton.
7 Bryan Robson. **8** Alan Shearer. **9** Billy Wright. **10** Gary Lineker.
11 Michael Owen. **12** David Beckham. **13** David Seaman.
14 He saved a penalty. **15** Gary Lineker. **16** David Platt. **17** Jimmy Greaves.
18 Bobby Moore. **19** Alan Shearer. **20** Steve McManaman. **21** Zagreb.
22 David Beckham. **23** Steven Gerrard. **24** Michael Owen. **25** John Terry.

QUIZ 5: *THREE LIONS 2 (page 178)* **1** QPR. **2** Stanley Matthews. **3** Once.
4 Gary Stevens. **5** They all scored. **6** Sweden. **7** Two. **8** Dixie Dean.
9 Viv Anderson. **10** Bobby Moore. **11** Nigeria. **12** Rangers. **13** Neil Webb.
14 Ian Wright. **15** Tom Finney. **16** David Platt. **17** Ray Wilson. **18** Emlyn.
19 84. **20** Stuart Pearce. **21** Tony Adams. **22** Luther Blissett (versus Luxembourg).
23 Five (Paul Bracewell, Gary Lineker, Peter Reid, Trevor Steven and Gary Stevens).
24 Danny Wallace. **25** Ukraine.

QUIZ 6: *ENGLAND POT LUCK (page 179)* **1** Belarus. **2** England 6, Andorra 0.
3 Theo Walcott. **4** Croatia. **5** Japan. **6** Six. **7** 1929. **8** 1953. **9** Ukraine away.
10 Sir Bobby Robson. **11** Scotland. **12** Barcelona. **13** Scotland.
14 Kennington Oval. **15** Lansdowne Road, Dublin. **16** 3–2 to Croatia.
17 Ray Clemence. **18** Richard Wright. **19** Eindhoven. **20** Frank Lampard.
21 Tony Kay, Francis Lee, Sammy Lee, Graham Rix. **22** Gordon Banks.
23 David James. **24** Alan Ball. **25** Qatar, UAE.

QUIZ 7: *WORLD CUP 2 (page 180)* **1** 1950. **2** USA. **3** 1–0. **4** Brazil.
5 Uruguay. **6** Uruguay. **7** Portugal. **8** 2–1 to England. **9** 1–0 to Brazil.
10 Three. **11** Paraguay. **12** Fourth. **13** Belgium. **14** 1–0 after extra-time.
15 Tunisia. **16** Paul Scholes. **17** Romania. **18** David Beckham. **19** 0–0.
20 St Etienne. **21** Bobby Robson. **22** West Germany 1974. **23** Mexico.
24 Gary Lineker. **5** Spain (1982).

QUIZ 8: *ENGLAND CAPTAINS (page 181)* **1** Bobby Moore. **2** Billy Wright.
3 Paul Ince. **4** Alan Shearer. **5** Johnny Haynes. **6** Eddie Hapgood.
7 David Platt. **8** Bryan Robson. **9** Peter Shilton. **10** Frank Swift.
11 Kevin Keegan. **12** Emlyn Hughes. **13** Jimmy Armfield.
14 Bryan Robson. **15** Ray Wilkins. **16** Mick Mills. **17** Gerry Francis.
18 Martin Peters. **19** Three times. **20** Ron Flowers. **21** Bobby Moore.
22 40 years. **23** Alan Shearer. **24** Jamie Carragher, Emile Heskey,
Phil Neville, Michael Owen. **25** John Terry.

QUIZ 9: *THREE LIONS 3 (page 182)* **1** 11. **2** Scotland. **3** Alan Mullery.
4 Peter Ward. **5** Three. **6** Tom Finney. **7** Brazil. **8** 53. **9** 90.
10 QPR & Manchester City. **11** Tony Adams. **12** Three. **13** Dave Watson.
14 European Championship 1988. **15** Jimmy Greaves. **16** 18 minutes.
17 73. **18** Tommy Lawton. **19** 1970. **20** Tony Cottee. **21** Wayne Rooney.
22 David Beckham. **23** 20. **24** Sol Campbell. **25** Peter Crouch.

QUIZ 10: *ENGLAND IN EUROPE (PAGE 183)* **1** Portugal. **2** 3–2 to Portugal.
3 Germany. **4** Alan Shearer. **5** Germany. **6** Switzerland. **7** 1–1.
8 Paul Gascoigne. **9** David Seaman. **10** Paul Scholes. **11** Terry Venables.
12 Spain. **13** Old Trafford. **14** Holland. **15** Romania. **16** Phil Neville.
17 Sweden. **18** 2–1 to Sweden. **19** Tomas Brolin. **20** The Golden Goal.
21 Portugal. **22** Alan Shearer. **23** Euro 1988. **24** France.
25 Portugal and Romania.

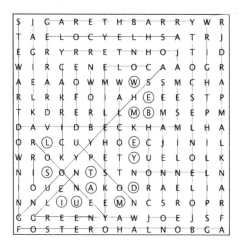

The unused letters spell out Wembley Stadium.

*ENGLAND
WORLD CUP
CROSSWORD 2*

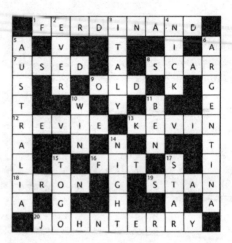

STAIRCASE CONUNDRUMS SOLUTIONS

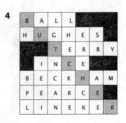